URBAN INDIANS

URBAN INDIANS

Donald L. Fixico
Western Michigan University

Frank W. Porter III
General Editor

CHELSEA HOUSE PUBLISHERS
New York Philadelphia

Frontispiece An Indian couple in downtown Minneapolis in 1981.

On the cover A detail of G. Peter Jemison's *Manhattan Fur Trade*, 31" × 23", 1984. *Manhattan Fur Trade* is part of a series of mixed-media works that explore the history of the 17th-century fur trade and its impact on New York City's economy. Jemison, a member of the Seneca tribe, lives in western New York State, where he manages the historic 17th-century Seneca townsite of Ganondagan.

Chelsea House Publishers
Editor-in-Chief Remmel Nunn
Managing Editor Karyn Gullen Browne
Copy Chief Juliann Barbato
Picture Editor Adrian G. Allen
Art Director Maria Epes
Deputy Copy Chief Mark Rifkin
Assistant Art Director Noreen Romano
Manufacturing Manager Gerald Levine
Systems Manager Lindsey Ottman
Production Manager Joseph Romano
Production Coordinator Marie Claire Cebrián

Indians of North America
Senior Editor Liz Sonneborn

Staff for **URBAN INDIANS**
Copy Editor Brian Sookram
Editorial Assistant Michele Haddad
Designer Debora Smith
Picture Researcher Sandy Jones

3 5 7 9 8 6 4 2

Library of Congress Cataloging-in-Publication Data

Fixico, Donald Lee
    Urban Indians/by Donald L. Fixico.
        p.   cm.—(Indians of North America)
    Includes bibliographical references and index.
    Summary: Examines the history, conditions, and changing fortunes of Indians living in urban America.
    ISBN 1-55546-732-6
        0-7910-0400-7 (pbk.)
    1. Indians of North America—Urban residence. 2. Indians of North America—Social conditions. [1. Indians of North America.] I. Title II. Series: Indians of North America (Chelsea House Publishers)
E98.U72F58 1991   90-49754
307.76'08997—dc20   CIP
                                                         AC

CONTENTS

INDIANS OF NORTH AMERICA

CHELSEA HOUSE PUBLISHERS

INDIANS OF NORTH AMERICA: CONFLICT AND SURVIVAL

Frank W. Porter III

> *The Indians survived our open intention of wiping them out, and since the tide turned they have even weathered our good intentions toward them, which can be much more deadly.*
>
> John Steinbeck
> *America and Americans*

When Europeans first reached the North American continent, they found hundreds of tribes occupying a vast and rich country. The newcomers quickly recognized the wealth of natural resources. They were not, however, so quick or willing to recognize the spiritual, cultural, and intellectual riches of the people they called Indians.

The Indians of North America examines the problems that develop when people with different cultures come together. For American Indians, the consequences of their interaction with non-Indian people have been both productive and tragic. The Europeans believed they had "discovered" a "New World," but their religious bigotry, cultural bias, and materialistic world view kept them from appreciating and understanding the people who lived in it. All too often they attempted to change the way of life of the indigenous people. The Spanish conquistadores wanted the Indians as a source of labor. The Christian missionaries, many of whom were English, viewed them as potential converts. French traders and trappers used the Indians as a means to obtain pelts. As Francis Parkman, the 19th-century historian, stated, "Spanish civilization crushed the Indian; English civilization scorned and neglected him; French civilization embraced and cherished him."

Nearly 500 years later, many people think of American Indians as curious vestiges of a distant past, waging a futile war to survive in a Space Age society. Even today, our understanding of the history and culture of American Indians is too often derived from unsympathetic, culturally biased, and inaccurate reports. The American Indian, described and portrayed in thousands of movies, television programs, books, articles, and government studies, has either been raised to the status of the "noble savage" or disparaged as the "wild Indian" who resisted the westward expansion of the American frontier.

Where in this popular view are the real Indians, the human beings and communities whose ancestors can be traced back to ice-age hunters? Where are the creative and indomitable people whose sophisticated technologies used the natural resources to ensure their survival, whose military skill might even have prevented European settlement of North America if not for devastating epidemics and disruption of the ecology? Where are the men and women who are today diligently struggling to assert their legal rights and express once again the value of their heritage?

The various Indian tribes of North America, like people everywhere, have a history that includes population expansion, adaptation to a range of regional environments, trade across wide networks, internal strife, and warfare. This was the reality. Europeans justified their conquests, however, by creating a mythical image of the New World and its native people. In this myth, the New World was a virgin land, waiting for the Europeans. The arrival of Christopher Columbus ended a timeless primitiveness for the original inhabitants.

Also part of this myth was the debate over the origins of the American Indians. Fantastic and diverse answers were proposed by the early explorers, missionairies, and settlers. Some thought that the Indians were descended from the Ten Lost Tribes of Israel, others that they were descended from inhabitants of the lost continent of Atlantis. One writer suggested that the Indians had reached North America in another Noah's ark.

A later myth, perpetrated by many historians, focused on the relentless persecution during the past five centuries until only a scattering of these "primitive" people remained to be herded onto reservations. This view fails to chronicle the overt and covert ways in which the Indians successfully coped with the intruders.

All of these myths presented one-sided interpretations that ignored the complexity of European and American events and policies. All left serious questions unanswered. What were the origins of the American Indians? Where did they come from? How and when did they get to the New World? What was their life—their culture—really like?

In the late 1800s, anthropologists and archaeologists in the Smithsonian Institution's newly created Bureau of American Ethnology in Washington,

8

D.C., began to study scientifically the history and culture of the Indians of North America. They were motivated by an honest belief that the Indians were on the verge of extinction and that along with them would vanish their languages, religious beliefs, technology, myths, and legends. These men and women went out to visit, study, and record data from as many Indian communities as possible before this information was forever lost.

By this time there was a new myth in the national consciousness. American Indians existed as figures in the American past. They had performed a historical mission. They had challenged white settlers who trekked across the continent. Once conquered, however, they were supposed to accept graciously the way of life of their conquerors.

The reality again was different. American Indians resisted both actively and passively. They refused to lose their unique identity, to be assimilated into white society. Many whites viewed the Indians not only as members of a conquered nation but also as "inferior" and "unequal." The rights of the Indians could be expanded, contracted, or modified as the conquerors saw fit. In every generation, white society asked itself what to do with the American Indians. Their answers have resulted in the twists and turns of federal Indian policy.

There were two general approaches. One way was to raise the Indians to a "higher level" by "civilizing" them. Zealous missionaries considered it their Christian duty to elevate the Indian through conversion and scanty education. The other approach was to ignore the Indians until they disappeared under pressure from the ever-expanding white society. The myth of the "vanishing Indian" gave stronger support to the latter option, helping to justify the taking of the Indians' land.

Prior to the end of the 18th century, there was no national policy on Indians simply because the American nation had not yet come into existence. American Indians similarly did not possess a political or social unity with which to confront the various Europeans. They were not homogeneous. Rather, they were loosely formed bands and tribes, speaking nearly 300 languages and thousands of dialects. The collective identity felt by Indians today is a result of their common experiences of defeat and/or mistreatment at the hands of whites.

During the colonial period, the British crown did not have a coordinated policy toward the Indians of North America. Specific tribes (most notably the Iroquois and the Cherokee) became military and political pawns used by both the crown and the individual colonies. The success of the American Revolution brought no immediate change. When the United States acquired new territory from France and Mexico in the early 19th century, the federal government wanted to open this land to settlement by homesteaders. But the Indian tribes that lived on this land had signed treaties with European governments assuring their title to the land. Now the United States assumed legal responsibility for honoring these treaties.

At first, President Thomas Jefferson believed that the Louisiana Purchase contained sufficient land for both the Indians and the white population. Within a generation, though, it became clear that the Indians would not be allowed to remain. In the 1830s the federal government began to coerce the eastern tribes to sign treaties agreeing to relinquish their ancestral land and move west of the Mississippi River. Whenever these negotiations failed, President Andrew Jackson used the military to remove the Indians. The southeastern tribes, promised food and transportation during their removal to the West, were instead forced to walk the "Trail of Tears." More than 4,000 men, woman, and children died during this forced march. The "removal policy" was successful in opening the land to homesteaders, but it created enormous hardships for the Indians.

By 1871 most of the tribes in the United States had signed treaties ceding most or all of their ancestral land in exchange for reservations and welfare. The treaty terms were intended to bind both parties for all time. But in the General Allotment Act of 1887, the federal government changed its policy again. Now the goal was to make tribal members into individual landowners and farmers, encouraging their absorption into white society. This policy was advantageous to whites who were eager to acquire Indian land, but it proved disastrous for the Indians. One hundred thirty-eight million acres of reservation land were subdivided into tracts of 160, 80, or as little as 40 acres, and allotted tribe members on an individual basis. Land owned in this way was said to have "trust status" and could not be sold. But the surplus land—all Indian land not allotted to individuals—was opened (for sale) to white settlers. Ultimately, more than 90 million acres of land were taken from the Indians by legal and illegal means.

The resulting loss of land was a catastrophe for the Indians. It was necessary to make it illegal for Indians to sell their land to non-Indians. The Indian Reorganization Act of 1934 officially ended the allotment period. Tribes that voted to accept the provisions of this act were reorganized, and an effort was made to purchase land within preexisting reservations to restore an adequate land base.

Ten years later, in 1944, federal Indian policy again shifted. Now the federal government wanted to get out of the "Indian business." In 1953 an act of Congress named specific tribes whose trust status was to be ended "at the earliest possible time." This new law enabled the United States to end unilaterally, whether the Indians wished it or not, the special status that protected the land in Indian tribal reservations. In the 1950s federal Indian policy was to transfer federal responsibility and jurisdiction to state governments, encourage the physical relocation of Indian peoples from reservations to urban areas, and hasten the termination, or extinction, of tribes.

Between 1954 and 1962 Congress passed specific laws authorizing the termination of more than 100 tribal groups. The stated purpose of the termination policy was to ensure the full and complete integration of Indians into American society. However, there is a less benign way to interpret this legislation. Even as termination was being discussed in Congress, 133 separate bills were introduced to permit the transfer of trust land ownership from Indians to non-Indians.

With the Johnson administration in the 1960s the federal government began to reject termination. In the 1970s yet another Indian policy emerged. Known as "self-determination," it favored keeping the protective role of the federal government while increasing tribal participation in, and control of, important areas of local government. In 1983 President Reagan, in a policy statement on Indian affairs, restated the unique "government is government" relationship of the United States with the Indians. However, federal programs since then have moved toward transferring Indian affairs to individual states, which have long desired to gain control of Indian land and resources.

As long as American Indians retain power, land, and resources that are coveted by the states and the federal government, there will continue to be a "clash of cultures," and the issues will be contested in the courts, Congress, the White House, and even in the international human rights community. To give all Americans a greater comprehension of the issues and conflicts involving American Indians today is a major goal of this series. These issues are not easily understood, nor can these conflicts be readily resolved. The study of North American Indian history and culture is a necessary and important step toward that comprehension. All Americans must learn the history of the relations between the Indians and the federal government, recognize the unique legal status of the Indians, and understand the heritage and cultures of the Indians of North America.

This ancient cliff dwelling, known as Cliff Palace, is located in the Mesa Verde National Park in Colorado. Built about 1,000 years ago by the Anasazi, Cliff Palace comprises plazas, ceremonial towers, and more than 220 rooms.

INDIAN CITIES
OF
YESTERDAY

When most Americans think of Indians in the United States today, they imagine people living on a reservation in isolation from the modern world. In fact, the majority of American Indians are residents of cities. According to the 1980 census, 63 percent of the Indian population of the United States inhabit urban areas.

In most ways, urban Indians' day-to-day lives are just like those of other American city dwellers. They live in apartments or houses, have jobs, attend school, read books, watch television, and go to restaurants, museums, parks, and movies. But, in other respects, urban Indians are unique. As Native Americans, they have a cultural heritage very different from that of Americans of European descent. Indian cultures were formed hundreds, in some cases even thousands, of years before Europeans traveled to North America. Indian people today continue to draw strength from the rich and ancient cultural legacy that links them to their ancestors. Unfortunately, however, this heritage has long sparked conflict between Indians and non-Indians, who throughout history have often misunderstood or even ridiculed Indian values and traditions.

City living is one of the many things urban Indians today have in common with their ancestors. Long before Indians had contact with whites, some Indian groups lived in vast, sophisticated urban centers. But owing to the different cultural traditions that created them, the early Indian cities little resembled those built by Europeans and Americans now and in the past. In general, ancient Indians tended to construct cities as centers of their religious life; European and American cities, in contrast, usually focus on economic activity.

The first Indian cities were established in Mesoamerica (now Guatemala, Belize, central and southern Mexico, and western Honduras and El Salvador). Although the date at which the first urban centers developed in that area is debated, cities were probably flourishing there at least 3,000 years ago. Perhaps as long as 4,000 years ago, native people were living in permanent villages in what is now the Valley of Mexico and Guatemala.

The urbanization of the Indians in Mesoamerica resulted from a great technological innovation—agriculture. When these early peoples learned how to farm crops such as maize (corn), squash, beans, and gourds, they no longer had to travel from place to place in search of wild animals and plants with which to feed themselves. Agriculture made it possible for them to stay in one location and live in the small permanent villages that eventually grew into cities.

In some areas, the agricultural system grew so productive that not all people needed to farm. Those who did not were free to perform other specialized tasks, such as making pottery, studying the stars, or organizing religious ceremonies. They could then trade goods or services to farmers in exchange for food. The result was a social system in which some people amassed more wealth than others and the population became segmented into

classes. Usually, there were large numbers of lower-class people whose labor was not needed to ensure a substantial food supply. The ruling elite, therefore, could afford to command such workers to construct massive public buildings to form the focus of major urban centers.

The earliest urban dwellers in present-day Mexico were the Olmec, the creators of the first civilization in the Americas. By about 1500 B.C., their society was flourishing. At centers such as San Lorenzo and La Venta, the Olmec constructed huge temple mounds and large religious sculptures. Locating their communities along trade routes, the Olmec were able to export their culture to other early peoples in the region before their civilization's decline.

Descended from the Olmec were the clever Maya people, who between A.D. 300 and 900 developed one of the greatest civilizations of the ancient world. At the height of the Maya's culture, approximately 116 Maya urban centers dotted what is now southern Mexico. Maya cities are more properly referred to as ceremonial centers because worship was the primary activity of the inhabitants' lives. These centers consisted of massive pyramids topped with temples, vast plazas used for public gatherings, and such other buildings as palaces, baths, and observatories. The size of the Maya's ceremonial centers varied greatly. The largest, Tikal, had about 100,000 residents; the smallest, Bonampak, was made up of only 11 modest buildings. Archaeological evidence found at these centers reveals that the

Temple I at the Maya ceremonial center of Tikal. The monumental structure was constructed in about A.D. 700.

Maya had advanced knowledge in mathematics and science. For instance, they developed a sophisticated calendar approximately 1,300 years before the Gregorian calendar used throughout the world today was created. The Maya also invented a system of numbers that used a zero. This mathematical innovation was not developed elsewhere until 1,000 years later when Hindus in India reinvented it.

Another great ancient urban center in the region was Teotihuacán, which was located in the middle of present-day Mexico. This large city, complete with suburbs, stretched over 20 square miles and probably had a population of at least 125,000. Like the Olmec and the Maya, the people of Teotihuacán built huge structures, which they decorated with carvings of serpents and other beasts and mythical feathered men.

Teotihuacán began to decline in about A.D. 750, possibly because of invasions of Toltec people. Several hundred years later, the Toltec established a powerful empire in the region. The Toltec's great city, Tula (also known as Tollum), was built high above a hilltop. The Toltec developed a reputation as master builders by filling this mighty center with palaces, pyramids, and ball courts.

Beginning in the 12th century, Indians who had migrated from the north gradually achieved dominance in central Mexico. In the 15th century, they allied themselves with neighboring groups to forge the Aztec Empire. The Aztec's greatest city was Tenochtitlán, which was located at the site of present-day Mexico City.

Early Spanish explorers who arrived in the area in the 16th century were amazed by the size and grandeur of Tenochtitlán. One Spaniard, Bernal Díaz del Castillo, later recorded their reaction.

> When we saw so many cities and villages built on the water and other great towns on dry land and that straight and level Causeway going toward Mexico [Tenochtitlán], we were amazed and said that it was like the enchantments they tell of in the legend of Amadis, on account of the great towers and cues [temples] and buildings rising from the water, and all built of masonry. And some of our soldiers even asked whether the things that we saw were not a dream.

In the center of the city was a huge walled plaza dominated by the massive temple of Huitzilopochtli and Tlaloc. Just outside the enclosure were large palaces for the Tenochtitlán elite. Farther out, approximately 80 residential districts housed the rest of the city's inhabitants. Each district had its own small plaza and temple.

During the same period, some Indian groups in various regions of the present-day United States developed urban centers, but none was as enormous as Tenochtitlán. Most of these northern communities housed only a few thousand people. One exception

The main ceremonial district of Tenochtitlán, reconstructed in a drawing by a 20th-century artist. The huge building to the left is the Great Temple of Huitzilopochtli and Tlaloc.

was Cahokia, located near what is now St. Louis, Missouri. At its height in about A.D. 1200, this trade and transportation center had a population of approximately 40,000 people.

Probably the best-known and most studied early American urban areas were those established by Indians in the Southwest. The Hohokam people living at the junction of the Gila and Salt rivers (now the location of Phoenix, Arizona) built elaborate irrigation systems that allowed them to farm in this region. By about A.D. 1000, they and the Anasazi people to the north had developed permanent villages that resembled those of their descendants, the Pueblo Indians.

One such urban center, Pueblo Bonito in Chaco Canyon of present-day New Mexico, shows the extent to which these peoples planned their cities. The population of Pueblo Bonito was highly concentrated. Its approximately 1,000 inhabitants lived in a complex of apartments that included 800 rooms, the largest apartment dwelling in existence until the 1880s.

By the end of the 15th century, when the first Europeans arrived in North America, small permanent urban

The remains of Pueblo Bonito in New Mexico's Chaco Canyon. In about 1070, the skillful Anasazi constructed this maze of dwellings for more than 1,000 people. It covers almost two acres.

centers existed among most agricultural Indian groups living within the current boundaries of the United States. For instance, the Iroquois and Huron of present-day New York State and southern Canada lived in palisaded villages and the tribal nations of large southeastern tribes, such as the Muscogee Creek and the Cherokee, were composed of a collection of towns. Even though the tribes of the Pacific Northwest generally obtained most of their food by fishing, their environment was so plentiful that they could stay in one place and still expect to have a constant food supply. They, too, formed permanent villages with sizable populations. As urban centers developed among all of these Indian peoples, their political, social, and religious systems adjusted to accommodate this type of living arrangement.

Although urbanization did not yet exist on a large scale among these groups, their towns and villages were growing when Europeans first came into their midst. Undoubtedly, urban areas populated by Indians would have increased in number and size if their development had not been interrupted by the arrival of these outsiders.

The first immigrants from the Old World came from Spain, France, the Netherlands, England, and Russia. Initially, most of these newcomers traveled to North and South America to obtain goods that they could export to

A drawing of an Iroquois village under siege, which originally appeared in the 1632 memoirs of French explorer Samuel de Champlain.

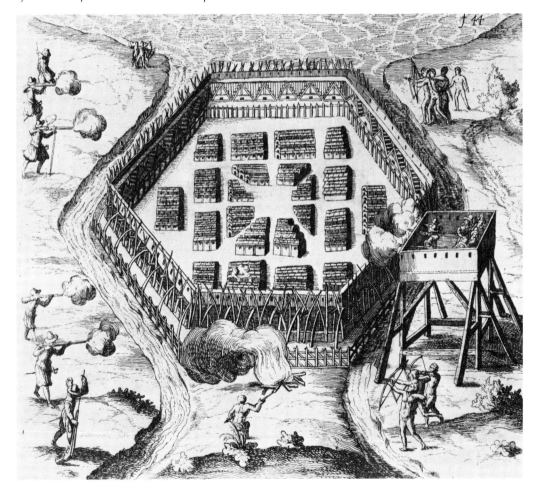

Europe and Russia for high profits. The exception were the English who, after the beginning of the 17th century, generally crossed the Atlantic Ocean with the intention of settling permanently in the New World.

Beginning in the early 1500s, the Spanish explored present-day South America, Mexico, and the southern region of the United States, cruelly exploiting the Indians living in these areas. Using Indian labor to mine for gold and silver, many of the early conquistadores amassed great fortunes. The Russians similarly mistreated the native peoples of what are now the Aleutian Islands, Alaska, the Canadian coast, and the northwestern United States. These explorers forced Indians and Aleuts into slavery, compelling them to hunt sea otters. Russians used the pelts of these animals to make warm fur coats.

The Indians' first contact with the French and the Dutch was friendlier. These Europeans were primarily interested in trading with the Indians of the New England coast and Great Lakes area for beaver pelts. The pelts were used for making hats and brought high prices in European markets. Because native hunters were skilled in trapping beavers, French and Dutch traders became convinced that it was in their best interests to establish a good business relationship with the Indians. To maintain trade relations, traders visited Indian villages and Indians traveled to colonial towns. Eventually some Indi-

ans took up permanent residence near the settlements of Europeans.

The white population of North America grew rapidly, especially in the settlements established by the English along the eastern seaboard. For a variety of reasons, many Europeans were eager to make the dangerous trip across

Many European settlers were lured to North America by the continent's rich environment. Unfortunately, most had little respect for Indians' claims to the land they occupied.

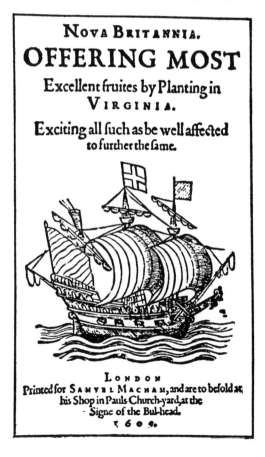

the ocean to establish a new life in the New World. The quest for wealth was certainly the driving factor for some; the desire for escape from the social and religious systems of their homeland was the motivation for others. But many were simply attracted by the New World's fertile farmland, abundant forests, and swift rivers and streams filled with fish. The vastness of this rich environment presented an opportunity previously unavailable to most Europeans. On their relatively small continent, only people of the wealthiest class could own land. In North America, however, there seemed to be plenty of land for everyone.

As more and more Europeans arrived in the New World, small settlements began to develop into towns and cities. Because of their residents' backgrounds, these urban areas resembled European cities more than cities and villages traditionally founded by North American Indians. By the 17th century, Boston, New York, Philadelphia, and Charlestown were thriving urban centers. In a relatively short time after contact, the largest cities in North America were those founded by non-Indians.

With the growth of colonial settlements, the European notion that North America was a virgin wilderness that belonged to whomever claimed it began to spell doom for many Indian cultures. The myth did not take into consideration that various Indian people had lived and hunted on this land for centuries. Unlike Europeans, Indians generally did not believe that individuals could own land. They did, however, recognize certain territories as the domain of certain Indian groups. Europeans simply ignored the rights of Indians to their traditional tribal territories and moved and established farms wherever they liked.

Indians often fought to keep Europeans off their land, but tribespeople were at a disadvantage in battling the settlers. While the European population was growing in North America, the Indian population was decreasing—primarily because the settlers had brought with them European diseases that killed Indian people in large numbers. Consequently, Indians were often outnumbered in conflicts with non-Indians. It was also difficult for Indians to organize a united assault on the foreigners. More than 350 tribes inhabited North America when Europeans began to arrive there. Many of these tribes were traditional enemies. Sometimes, a tribe that regarded the European settlers as a threat may have hated and feared its Indian neighbors even more. Many Indian leaders tried to form Indian alliances against the white invaders, but because of the differences between the many Indian groups, none was totally successful.

Animosity among Indian peoples increased as European colonies expanded westward. The settlers often moved onto Indian land and displaced the native population. The displaced Indians then had to move westward

themselves into the territory of other Indians, who resented and often battled the newcomers. Whether a tribal territory was invaded by Europeans or by other Indian peoples, the tribe's society was affected. With foreigners in their midst, an Indian group's entire world changed. To adapt, they were compelled to alter or even abandon many of their traditional ways of living.

One of the earliest casualties of traditional Indian cultures was their urban

The city of New York as it appeared in about 1667.

centers. Unlike European cities, which were shaped by the political, industrial, and religious events that occurred in nearby areas, Indian cities had developed fairly independently. Indian urban centers were so geographically isolated that they traditionally had little effect on one another. This isolation helped to draw the inhabitants of Indian cities together, but it also made the cities ill equipped to deal with change. When Europeans and foreign Indians moved into an Indian urban center, the city tended to fall into decline rather than change to cope with the newcomers.

By the time of the American Revolution, much of the Indian territory east of the Mississippi was overrun by non-Indians. After the war ended in victory for the American colonists, the government of the newly formed United States soon began to develop policies regarding the treatment of the Indians living within its boundaries. Like their ancestors, the American policymakers discounted the Indians' rights to the territory they had occupied for centuries. Instead of seeing whites as the invaders of Indian land, U.S. officials viewed the native peoples of North America as foreigners. The thrust of the United States's Indian policy for the next 100 years would be to eliminate the threat posed by these "outsiders" in either of 2 ways—by making Indians behave like whites or by forcing Indians to leave the land that non-Indians had shamelessly claimed as their own. ▲

Richard Pratt, founder of the Carlisle Industrial Training School, and a group of Navajo Indians photographed upon their arrival at the institution.

A CENTURY
OF
DISRUPTION

In 1803, President Thomas Jefferson bought, on behalf of the United States, the stretch of land between the Mississippi River and the Rocky Mountains from France. Known as the Louisiana Purchase, this vast tract doubled the size of the United States, providing its people with land and resources that would eventually help the country to become a major world power. But at the time of the purchase, Jefferson knew little about what he was buying. He was not thinking as much about how the land might be used by Americans as how it could help solve the "Indian problem." The president hoped to persuade the Indians who still lived east of the Mississippi, especially those in the Southeast, to leave their homelands and relocate west of the river. Then, American settlers could have free access to the rich lands these Indians had traditionally occupied.

The idea of relocating, or removing, Indians to the West was a priority of the government for the next few decades. But it was not until the passage of the Indian Removal Act of 1830 that the policy was put into practice on a large scale. Indians strongly resisted removal, but representatives of the government, often by deceptive or illegal means, generally were able to coax tribal leaders to sign treaties in which they agreed to sell their homeland and move to Indian Territory, originally a loosely defined area in what is today Nebraska, Kansas, and Oklahoma.

Some supporters of removal claimed that the policy would save the eastern Indians' culture by isolating Indians from white society. In fact, it was enormously disruptive to traditional Indian ways. Large, once powerful tribes such as the Cherokee, the Muscogee Creek, and the Choctaw were compelled to abandon their homes and move hundreds of miles away to an environment very different from that which they had always known. Usually, the removal of entire tribal populations of thousands of people took place in only a matter of years.

As best they could, the removed Indians tried to rebuild their societies, often establishing towns with the same names as those their ancestors had founded in the Southeast. But, not surprisingly, their adjustment to the West was difficult. The land in much of their new territory, especially in the portion to the east, was arid and hard to farm. They were also sometimes attacked by Indians native to the Great Plains because much of the land granted to the removed Indians was part of the Plains Indians' traditional territory. The government agreed to protect the removed Indians from Plains Indian attacks but rarely made good on these promises.

In their treaties with the U.S. government, the removed tribes were also guaranteed that their new homelands would be theirs forever. However, the coming of railroads to Indian Territory in the 1870s threatened Indians' control over the region. Railroads made the West much more accessible. Whites could easily board a train and head westward to seek their fortune. Huge numbers of non-Indians soon began to arrive in Indian Territory, often after hearing rumors about available farmland.

This large influx of whites encroached not only on the land of the

Throughout the 19th century, federal Indian policy aided non-Indians seeking to gain control of Indian land. This 1879 poster advertises the opening of land in Indian Territory (now Oklahoma) to white settlers.

removed Indians but also on the traditional territory of the Plains tribes. Many Plains Indian groups, such as the Apache and the Comanche, warred with U.S. soldiers sent to protect the white invaders of the Indians' homelands. In the end, these Indians were defeated in what became known as the Plains Wars. In their peace treaties with the United States, most were forced to surrender their territory and relocate to small tracts that were a fraction of the size of their homelands. These tracts, called reservations, were to be settled only by Indians.

The government claimed that by isolating Indians on reservations it was protecting them and their culture from destruction. In truth, the policy enabled the United States to gain control over an enormous amount of formerly Indian-occupied territory. Also, by concentrating Indians in small areas, the government could police their activities and quickly suppress any further Indian rebellions.

Although the culture of the Plains Indians was based on hunting buffalo, once Indians were confined to reservations, U.S. officials expected them to become farmers. Most reservation land was infertile, however, and their confinement rendered them unable to obtain food through their traditional means. Thus, many reservation Indians came to depend on rations from the U.S. government for their very survival.

Rations were often distributed at local offices of the Bureau of Indian Affairs (BIA), the department of the federal government charged with dealing with all Indian groups. Around these offices, which were known as agencies, small urban centers often grew up. Although they had many Indian residents, these centers were not like Indian towns and cities of the past. Their development was not guided by the Indians' cultural traditions. Instead, they were essentially centers of economic activity. In this way, these new "Indian" cities were similar to American and European urban areas.

The growth of these reservation urban areas was furthered by missionaries. With the permission of the federal government, missionaries often lived among reservation Indians in the hope of converting them to Christianity. They generally built schools and churches—the centers of their conversion efforts—close to agency offices. Consequently, much of the population of towns such as St. Francis in South Dakota and St. Michael in Arizona were Christianized Indians. Tensions sometimes grew between these urban Indians who adopted many of the values as well as the religion of non-Indians and the more traditional residents of the same reservation.

At the same time that agency towns grew up, some reservation Indians began to frequent non-Indian urban centers that had developed along railroad lines or in areas where prospectors flocked in search of gold and silver. In these frontier towns, Indians often had their first sustained contact with non-

A group of Quechan Indians in the town of Yuma, Arizona. In the late 19th century, towns and cities founded by non-Indians near reservations became social and economic centers for Indians as well.

Indians. After visiting these areas, some chose to stay, particularly those who could find wage work. Most Indian visitors were not warmly welcomed, however. Although the Plains Wars were over, there remained a great deal of hostility between Indians and non-Indians.

Throughout the late 19th century, living conditions on most reservations deteriorated. Even though its treaties with Indians usually obliged the U.S. government to provide food and supplies to Indians for a certain period of time following their relocation, the government often went back on its promise. Left with inadequate rations, large numbers of reservation inhabitants died of starvation or disease.

The deplorable state of reservation life led some influential people to demand changes in federal Indian policy.

These reformers pointed out that if the reservation policy had intended to protect Indians, it was a dismal failure. They claimed that the only way reservation Indians could survive was to become self-sufficient and assimilated—that is, to adopt the values and behavior of whites.

The assimilation of Indians into white society had long been a goal of missionaries in North America. In addition to converting Indians to Christianity, they often tried to teach Indians the ways of whites. Establishing schools for Indian children was one of the most effective ways of transmitting white culture to tribal groups.

The U.S. government developed boarding schools for the same purpose in the late 19th century. Indian children

Two ration tickets issued in 1884 to Teton Sioux Indians living on the Pine Ridge Indian Reservation in South Dakota. Unable to obtain food through traditional means, reservation Indians often became dependent on rations from the federal government.

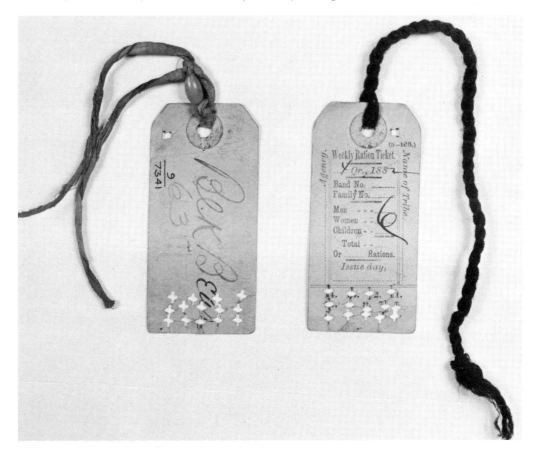

Photographs of Navajo Tom Toslino when he came to Carlisle (left) and three years after his arrival. Carlisle officials used such before-and-after pictures to gain support for the school's goal of assimilating Indians into white society.

were often forcibly taken from their parents and sent to live at schools hundreds of miles away from their homes. Officials in the BIA believed that separating the students from their culture would ensure that the children learned and adopted white values. Richard Pratt, the founder of the Carlisle Industrial Training School in Pennsylvania, went one step further. He established an "outing" program through which students lived with white families in nearby communities rather than in dormatories. By working on a family's farm or doing its household chores, the Indian boys and girls experienced firsthand the way of life of white people.

The BIA strongly supported the boarding-school system, but most Indians opposed it. Parents were outraged when their children were taken from them against their will. Mistreated by their teachers, students often ran away from school. Even children who displayed less resistance to assimilation were not well served. Although when they left their boarding schools they knew how to act like whites, they could not feel comfortable in white society because whites still regarded them as Indian savages. The assimilated young people could fit in no better with their own people. Trained to respect white values, they had come to feel like strangers within their own family.

Another policy advocated by reformers to aid assimilation was known as allotment. Traditionally, Indian groups held their land in common; no one was regarded as the owner of any particular portion of the group's territory. Allotment supporters sought to end this central element of Indians' culture. The reformers believed that if Indians were allowed to own small plots and were given farming tools and seeds, then they would have more incentive to work their land. Also, they expected that if native people became landowners like their white neighbors, they would, over time, adopt other aspects of white culture as well.

The U.S. government had still other reasons for supporting allotment. In the 1880s, influential officials were concerned about the large sums the government spent on the rations and services it provided for Indians according to past treaties. If Indians became self-sufficient farmers, the officials could justify cutting, and eventually stopping altogether, their aid to Indians. Allotment also made it possible for the United States to gain control over more Indian land. According to the General Allotment Act of 1887, which provided for the allotment of many reservations across the country, individual Indians received legal title to a plot (called an allotment) of between 40 and 160 acres of their tribe's land. If the tribe had a small population and a large territory, a great deal of land was left over after all allotments had been assigned. This "surplus" land then became the property of the government, which usually opened it up for white settlement. The direct result of the General Allotment Act was to dispossess Indians of most of the little land they still retained in the late 19th century. In the 50 years following the passage of the act, the amount of land owned by Indians fell from 138 million to 48 million acres.

The allotment policy failed to help Indians become self-sufficient. Many Indians who were given allotments did not want to be farmers, and many of those who did found their plot too small and too infertile to support a family. The basic premise that Indians could become successful small farmers at this time was also marred. By the end of the 19th century, sophisticated agricultural tools and techniques had made large-scale farming increasingly profitable. As time went by, small farms found it harder and harder to compete with these larger operations. In addition, industry began overtaking agriculture as the foundation of the United States's economy. Thus, forcing a farming way of life on Indians during this period was far from the best strategy for preparing them to make a living in the years to come.

Instead of making Indians part of mainstream America, the government's policies rendered them the most impoverished minority group in the country. At the beginning of the 20th century, most reservation Indians remained destitute. They were, however, able to draw strength from living in traditional Indian communities and being guided by traditional Indian leaders. Many Indians who had received allotments had neither of these comforts. With the allotment of their tribe's ter-

In the late 19th century, federal officials debated how best to assimilate Indians. This political cartoon by Thomas Nast shows Secretary of the Interior Carl Schurz explaining the voting process to a group of Indians. The caption calls giving Indians the vote "the cheapest and quickest way of civilizing them."

ritory, their communities had dissolved and the United States had disbanded their tribal governments.

Reservation Indians also had an economic advantage over allottees. Indians living on reservations were still entitled to goods and services due to them according to past treaties. Allottees, on the other hand, generally were not.

With their allotments, some had received U.S. citizenship, a benefit the government believed compensated for the loss of government services. However, citizenship did Indians little good. They could vote, but because of their relatively small numbers, they essentially had no power to elect officials who would look after their interests.

The United States had long regarded assimilation and the receipt of government aid as incompatible. In 1879, the Supreme Court's decision in the lawsuit *Standing Bear v. Crook* held that Indians could choose to leave their reservations to live in white communities, but that they would then lose their eligibility for government support.

This view was reinforced in 1928 with the publication of *The Problem of Indian Administration*, which interpreted the results of a federal government study of the living conditions of Indians. For 7 months, 9 researchers visited 75 reservations and collected data. Their findings, edited by Lewis Meriam and popularly known as the Meriam Report, disclosed that the state of health care, education, and the economy in Indian communities was hor-

Commissioner of Indian Affairs John C. Collier photographed with the chiefs of the Blackfeet Indians in 1934. Collier advocated the end of the allotment policy and the return of tribalism.

rendous. The report placed much of the blame for these conditions on the government's past policies and was particularly disparaging of allotment. The Meriam Report stated that "it almost seems as if the government assumed that some magic in individual ownership of property would in itself prove an educational, civilizing factor." The "outing" program at Carlisle was another of the document's targets. It charged that the children who were forced to participate in it were ill prepared to live in white society.

The Meriam Report recommended a number of significant reforms in federal Indian policy. It called for the end of allotment and for the establishment of Indian day schools on or close to reservations. The report also argued that the meager sums Indian communities received from the federal government were not enough to help them develop economically.

The Meriam Report, however, did not recommend the establishment of any special programs for "migrated Indians"—its term for Indians who had chosen to sell their allotments and move to cities or former boarding-school students who never returned home. Instead, the study's findings suggested that the federal government work with existing city social agencies to help the Indians in their area. The idea that the welfare of urban Indians was, for the most part, the responsibility of the city in which they resided would continue to pull weight throughout the 20th century.

John C. Collier, who headed the BIA from 1933 to 1945, took the recommendations of the Meriam Report to heart. He was a great advocate of tribalism—that is, the maintenance of traditional Indian ways of life—and agreed that allotment had hurt many Indian people. Largely owing to Collier's efforts, Congress passed the Indian Reorganization Act (IRA) in 1934, which officially ended the allotment policy. The act also set down guidelines for the reformation of tribal governments and put aside funds for loans for the economic development of tribes.

Collier's critics felt that he wanted to reform Indian affairs too quickly. They complained that it made little sense to allow Indians to return to traditionalism when so much effort had gone into making them assimilate. They failed to see what Collier did see—that Indians' culture brought great strength to their communities. Collier believed that the best way to improve the Indians' lot was to make use of this strength rather than to continue to undermine it.

The IRA helped improve the economic conditions of Indians across the nation. Ironically, its benefits were first felt when most other Americans were suffering from the effects of the Great Depression. Indians were relatively untouched by the downturn in the nation's economy in the 1930s because they were already impoverished.

One exception was the Indians of Oklahoma. A severe drought caused their farmland to be too dry to be productive. Like their non-Indian neigh-bors, many left the region and headed West. A large number of these migrants found new homes in California, espe-cially in Los Angeles. (This migration helps to account for Los Angeles' large Indian population, the greatest of any American city today.)

Another group of Indians who had experiences in urban centers during the Great Depression were laborers in the Indian Division of the Civilian Conser-vation Corps (CCC). The federal gov-ernment formed the CCC in 1933 to combat unemployment throughout the United States. The corps hired people to construct schools, libraries, dams, roads, and other public facilities. The Indian men who found work through the CCC usually had to leave their com-munity for an extended period of time. When they came home they brought, along with their paychecks, informa-tion about the urban centers they had

seen. Hearing news of jobs in towns and cities, some Indians chose to relo-cate. Again, California, where work was available picking fruits and vege-tables, was the destination for many.

Most reservation Indians, however, chose to remain in their communities during the economic hard times. Few had the money to leave, and gradually IRA funds were giving them more in-centive to stay. From removal to the res-ervation policy to allotment, the federal Indian policies of the past 100 years had had the effect of constantly uprooting Indian people. Finally the United States was lending support to Indians' efforts to retain a tribal way of life. The return of tribalism, though, would be short-lived. With the bombing of Pearl Har-bor on December 7, 1941, Indians, like all other Americans, would be swept up into a period of great change as the United States was drawn into World War II. ▲

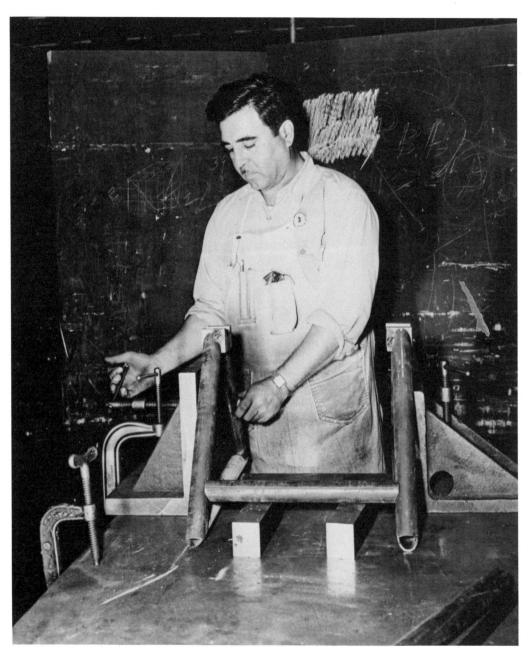

Adolph Bell, an Arikara Indian, working in a factory in Los Angeles in 1953. Bell was one of the first relocation applicants at the BIA's office in Aberdeen, South Dakota.

THE
RELOCATION POLICY

In 1924, all American Indians were granted citizenship. Therefore, as U.S. citizens, Indian men were subject to the draft during World War II. However, before they were called, many eagerly volunteered for military service. Some elderly Navajo men even asked at a BIA office where they could go to enlist, and the Iroquois Nation went so far as to declare war on Germany.

Why Indians were so willing to fight for the same country that had cheated them out of their homelands was unclear to many non-Indians. In fact, Indians' past experiences with the U.S. government probably played a role in persuading Indian youths to sign up for the military services. In a sense, they were merely following a long tradition of fighting to defend their territory. Only the enemy had changed. In the past, many of their ancestors had bat-

tled U.S. soldiers. Now Indians themselves were U.S. soldiers charged with battling German and Japanese troops.

Some Indians, however, had more personal reasons for enlisting. A number of volunteers were inspired by older male relatives who had served in World War I. Others saw military service in World War II as their last chance to become distinguished warriors, a role that traditionally was revered in many Indian cultures.

All told, 25,000 Indian men and 500 Indian women joined the U.S. armed services during the war. Many received respect and praise for their valor. Two Indian servicemen, Lieutenant Ernest Childers and Lieutenant Jack C. Montgomery, were awarded congressional medals, the most distinguished decoration conferred by the United States for military heroism. The Navajo

Esther Quintan Cheshewalla of the Osage tribe was one of the first Indian women to join the U.S. Marine Corps during World War II.

Codetalkers were also singled out for praise by the federal government. On battlefields in the Pacific, these soldiers communicated messages in a code in the Navajo language. The complexities of the Navajo language prevented the Japanese from deciphering the code.

The distinguished performance of Indian troops was matched by Indian civilians. Between 40,000 and 50,000 Indian men and women took jobs in industries that produced items needed in wartime, such as uniforms, jeeps, and steel. Some commuted from their res-ervations to nearby factories. Others left their homes and moved to non-Indian communities to work in war industries.

The routine of all Americans was disrupted by World War II, but Indians were affected especially deeply. The war years marked the first time many Indian soldiers and civilians had ever left their Indian community. With their introduction to the world outside their reservation, they were confronted with a host of foreign values, different viewpoints, new ideologies, and divergent philosophies. For people who adhered closely to tribal traditions, this sudden exposure to the ways of non-Indians amounted to culture shock. Even Indians who did not go to war or work at war jobs were indirectly influenced. They learned about American cities, Europe, and Japan from the stories of friends and relatives who had seen these places for themselves.

Toward the end of the war, American Indians began to address their common problems and concerns. In 1944, delegates representing many tribes called a meeting in Denver, Colorado, to form the National Congress of American Indians (NCAI) to deal with Indian issues in response to past injustices and future treatment from the federal government. The NCAI has since met annually to discuss problems Indians share and possible solutions.

When the war ended in 1945, many Indian soldiers returned to their reservations only to face another traumatic cultural conflict. Their experiences in

Like these Sioux men, many of the approximately 25,000 Indians in the U.S. armed services during the war were volunteers.

other parts of the world had changed them. Like boarding-school graduates decades before, they no longer felt at home on the reservation, but they also did not feel wholly comfortable outside it. They were aliens both in their own Indian communities and in mainstream American society. Unsure of what to do, many Indian veterans drifted toward towns and large cities to begin new lives.

The economic conditions of Indian communities convinced other veterans to move away. Despite IRA funding, a limited number of jobs available on or near most reservations gave them no choice but to migrate to cities where job opportunities were greater. They were followed by some Indians who, now trained in factory work, felt confident that they could compete with non-Indians for industrial jobs in urban areas.

The federal government took note of the migration of Indians to cities in the years immediately following the war. John Collier, who resigned his post as commissioner of Indian affairs in 1945, declared that "the war has brought about the greatest exodus of Indians from reservations that has ever taken place." A news release from the Department of the Interior reported:

> World War II demonstrated to many Indians who participated in the various phases of its activities, both in the armed services and in defense industries, the futility of attempting to maintain an isolated system of primitive community life. The outside world did offer to the participating Indians exciting, desirable and worthwhile possibilities for individual achievement.

Certainly the majority of American Indians, who remained in Indian communities, did not share the government's view that their efforts to preserve their traditions were futile; nor did they see the outside world as offering much that was more desirable or worthwhile than the elements of their own culture. Although Indians did not share the government's view that mainstream society was superior in all ways to traditional Indian cultures, most other Americans did.

During the war, American people of all races and backgrounds had worked together to defeat common enemies. Despite their differences, they were in

Four Indian teenagers photographed in Central Park during a visit to New York City in 1949. In the years immediately following World War II, many reservation Indians traveled to urban areas for the first time.

many ways very much the same. When the conflict was over, many Americans wanted to forget about the things that separated the American people and to emphasize what they had in common. In this intellectual climate, "foreign" values or customs were sometimes branded as "un-American." Indians' emphasis on the community over the individual, for instance, came under attack.

In the 1930s, the Indian Reorganization Act had tried to restore the tribalism that the allotment policy had sought to destroy in the 19th century. Now, in the early 1950s, the U.S. government began to consider another change in its federal Indian policy. Instead of attempting to support Indians' efforts to retain their traditional ways, the U.S. officials again wanted to compel them to live like non-Indian Americans. This goal was articulated in the House Concurrent Resolution 108, which was approved by Congress with little discussion in 1953. The resolution stated:

> Whereas it is the policy of Congress, as rapidly as possible, to make the Indians within the territorial limits of the United States subject to the same laws and entitled to the same privileges and responsibilities as are applicable to other citizens of the United States, and to end their status as wards of the United States, and to grant them all of the rights and prerogatives pertaining to American citizenship.

Simply put, the United States wanted to terminate Indian lands' trust status and to stop providing tribes with the financial support and services that it had promised to give them in past treaties.

The government had begun preparing to terminate its economic responsibilities to tribes in the late 1940s by establishing the Indian Claims Commission. Any Indian group that felt it had been treated unfairly by the United States in the past could present its case before the commission. Most of the complaints involved the United States's illegal and immoral seizure of Indian land. The total financial settlements made by the commission eventually amounted to more than $800 million. The government contended that this compensation justified terminating all legal and financial obligations to Indian peoples.

The seeds of another important new U.S. Indian policy began in the late 1940s. In the winter of 1947–48, severe blizzards struck the Navajo Indian Reservation in northern Arizona. Freezing and starving, Navajo Indians in isolated areas were saved by emergency shipments of food and supplies. The publicity surrounding the event aroused both public and government concern for the Navajo. It became clear that, even when not in time of emergency, the Navajo people were not faring well.

Mired in poverty, the Navajo suffered from poor living conditions and rampant disease. In 1946, it was esti-

IRA HAYES:
HEROIC SOLDIER, TROUBLED VETERAN

In one of the most famous photographs taken during World War II, six U.S. soldiers are shown raising an American flag on Iwo Jima after marines drove the Japanese from the Pacific island. The picture, taken by Joe Rosenthal, won a Pulitzer Prize, was widely reproduced, and inspired a statue that now stands outside Arlington National Cemetery. During and after the war, the image became a symbol of American courage and valor.

Among the flag raisers at Iwo Jima was Marine Private First Class Ira Hayes, a Pima Indian from Arizona. Hayes also became a symbol. His heroic efforts in Japan came to represent the bravery displayed by the thousands of Indian men and women who joined the U.S. military services during the war.

Hayes's fame was no accident. Seeing him as a good spokesman for the government's campaign to sell the U.S. bonds that helped finance the war, U.S. officials removed the private from combat duty and sent him on tour across the United States. The army promoted him as a virtuous "red man" who had acted as a "noble warrior" in hopes that his story would inspire patriotism in other Americans.

The raising of the American flag on Iwo Jima, photographed by Joe Rosenthal in 1943.

Ira Hayes in uniform, 1945.

Hayes was never at ease with the vast amount of media attention he received. He was even less comfortable when he returned to his homeland. Feeling out of place among his people after his wartime experiences, he fell victim to alcoholism. Having endured ferocious battles in the Pacific yet unable to survive his alienation at home, Hayes died in 1955.

Hayes's celebrity among Indian veterans was unique. Unfortunately, his desperation following the war was not. Many of Hayes's fellow veterans felt lost in their old communities and traveled to cities to seek a new way of life. Some adapted well, but others—feeling just as out of place in the city as on the reservation—found themselves between two worlds, unable to call either one home.

In the winter of 1947–48, blizzards struck Navajo country. Thousands of dollars of emergency aid were spent to provide relief to people living in isolated areas of the tribe's reservation.

mated that only 5,300 of the 11,000 Navajo families owned arable land. The families that were able to farm could not earn a decent income from their efforts; on the average, they produced only $189 worth of crops per year. Just as many other Americans were not sympathetic to the plight of Indian veterans after the war, during this period some uninformed people criticized the Navajo for not being more productive, unaware of the historic conditions that had created the Indians' poverty. For instance, when one Navajo went to a Red Cross office to apply for aid, an office worker asked him:

> "Why don't you get a job?"
> "I can't. I feel tired all the time," replied the Indian.
> "I can't put that on the record. What do you mean?" the worker asked.
> "Well you see—sometimes I don't eat for two or three days," the Navajo said.

BIA officials acknowledged that the Navajo needed help. The economy of their reservation was stagnant but this was only part of the problem. The Navajo population was growing. If the Navajo Indians were to avoid sinking even further into poverty, it was clear that one of two things would have to happen: Either their reservation economy would have to improve to support the additional people, or some Navajo would have to move to areas where jobs were already available. Because financial aid to bolster the Navajo economy

would be very expensive, the BIA opted in 1948 to develop a program to encourage Navajo Indians to relocate to urban areas. Having in mind the example of the many Indian veterans who had already chosen to leave their reservation communities, the officials reasoned that the program would merely help Indians to make a move that they were already eager to make.

The BIA's relocation program began on a small scale. Relocation officers were assigned to Los Angeles, California; Denver, Colorado; and Salt Lake City, Utah. They tried to find employers in these areas who would be willing to hire Navajo Indians for temporary or permanent jobs. When they did, they notified BIA officials on the Navajo reservation, who passed along the information to interested Indians.

Considering the program a success, the BIA in 1949 requested and received funds from Congress to extend its job placement services. Officers were hired to help find jobs for Indians living in or near Aberdeen, South Dakota; Billings, Montana; and Portland, Oregon. In 1951, the BIA extended relocation services in Oklahoma, New Mexico, California, Arizona, Utah, and Colorado and opened a field office in Chicago.

Each successive year, the BIA asked for larger sums for the program. In 1952, Congress allocated slightly more than $500,000, enough money to extend the program to serve Indians across the nation. The commissioner of Indian affairs, Dillon Myer, then created a new branch of the BIA dedicated to what

This Navajo woman applied for relocation in the late 1950s and subsequently moved to Denver, Colorado. She found work in a saddle factory, weaving cinches decorated with Indian-style designs.

became known as "relocation services." In that year alone, 442 Indians found employment in Los Angeles, Denver, and Chicago through the efforts of relocation workers.

Commissioner Myer had great expectations for the relocation program. To fund its growth, he asked Congress in 1953 for $8.5 million. Myer argued that the money was needed to finance job training programs for relocatees (Indians who relocated to urban areas). With the exception of those who had worked in wartime industries, most reservation Indians had little education or training that would qualify them for

continued on page 57

THE NEW INDIAN ART

Until recently, most contemporary Indian artists drew inspiration from traditional artwork and craftwork. But in the 1960s, a new type of Indian artist began to emerge. This artist felt less restricted to using the forms and materials employed by older Indian artisans and more comfortable exploring techniques associated with Western art.

In the face of these changes, many Indian painters and sculptors are reexamining the meaning of "Indian art." Just as living among non-Indians compels urban Indians to explore and often redefine the nature of Indianness, increased exposure to Western art has made recent Indian artists ask what unifies their own works. Does Indian art refer to art made by people of Indian ancestry? Or does it include only works that are made using old Indian techniques and materials? Or is it art's subject matter that makes it Indian?

On the following pages appear examples of the work of three urban Indian artists—Lloyd E. Oxendine, Peter Horne Sarabella, and Diosa M. Summers. All these pieces have been exhibited at the American Indian Community House Gallery/ Museum, the only Indian-owned gallery in New York City. Some are representational; others are abstract. Some communicate information about the lives of Indians today or long ago; others have no overt Indian theme. Some hark back to works made by past Indian artists; others show the influence of non-Indian art.

The diversity of these works clearly illustrates the difficulty of arriving at a simple explanation of what makes contemporary Indian art "Indian." But in their variety there is another lesson: By combining the new and the old, Indian artists are discovering inventive ways to express the multitude of things being Indian can mean today.

Lloyd E. Oxendine's Prayer, 25" x 37", 1987.

Right: *Detail from* Overseer of the Golden Planet, *56" x 66", 1987.*

Lloyd E. Oxendine, a Lumbee Indian, is the curator of the American Indian Community House Gallery/Museum in New York City and a frequent lecturer on contemporary Indian art.

Barbed Wire, Prairie, Grass, *24½" x 30½", 1986.*

Tribute to Liberty, *32″ x 44″, 1987.*

Old Indian Story, *56″ x 66″, 1987.*

Birth of the Iroquois, *20'' x 30'' x 8''*, *1989.*

Broken Promises, 36" x
30" x 6", 1987.

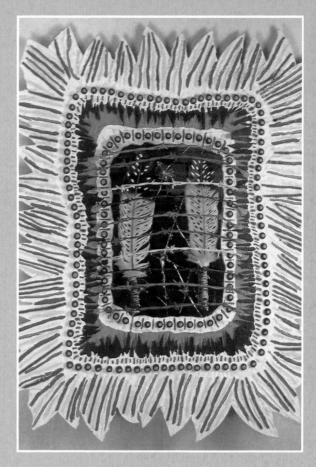

*A resident of Long Island,
New York, Peter Horne Sarabella is of combined Mo-
hawk and Italian-American
ancestry. According to the
artist, his work is created
from "whatever materials
seem useful."*

Birth Chorus, 36" x 48" x
7", 1987.

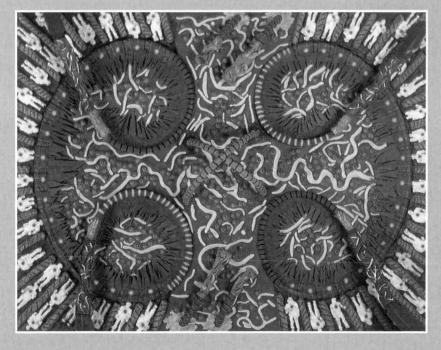

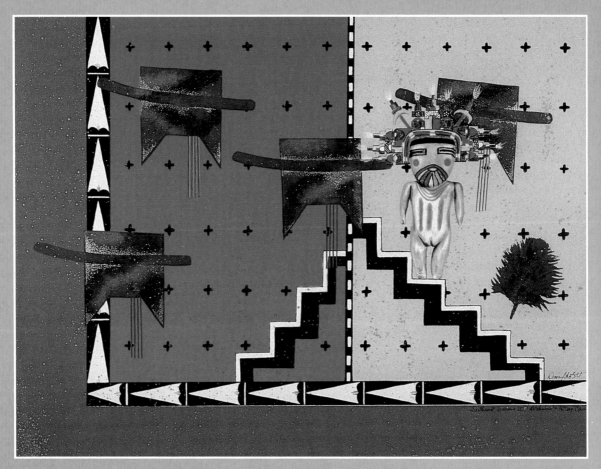

Southwest Visions, 23″ x
30″, 1989.

Horses, 18″ x 24″, 1990.

Diosa M. Summers—a resident of Staten Island, New York, and a member of the Mississippi band of Choctaw—teaches Native American art history at Parsons School of Design and has directed arts education programs in several museums in New York City. Of her art she says, "I only hope that as I look within my visions . . . as I look at the happy things, the wonderthings, the beautythings the Creator has given us . . . I can show the world the preciousness of it all. I try to do this with my artwork, and hopefully make people aware, and obsessed with my obsession, too."

Below: Ghost Dance, *22" x 30", 1989.*

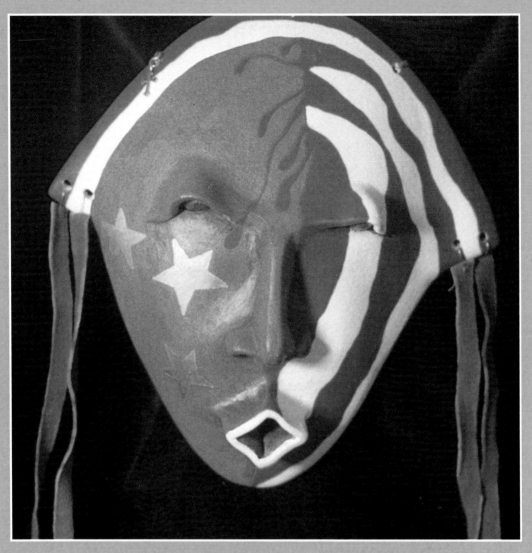

Diosa M. Summers' My Country Tis of Thee, *ceramic painted with acrylic, 11"*
x 9", 1989. According to the author, "The symbol of the U.S. government has a
life; it brings with it tears and blood, while it represents itself as a familiar,
friendly entity."

continued from page 48

well-paying jobs. Congress did not see the need for the massive vocational training program Myer wanted to establish and therefore allocated only a little more than $500,000 to relocation—about one-seventeenth of the funds Myer had requested.

Even with Congress's hesitant support, the relocation program continued to grow. Initially, both the BIA and many Indians cheered it as a means for poor Indians to improve their standard of living. Some critics, though, saw relocation as the BIA's way of abandoning the Indian people. They claimed that once Indians became city dwellers the government would try to cut off all the services the BIA had provided them in the past.

At first, few Indians wanted to volunteer for relocation. Gradually, though, stories of the adventures of

An Indian man signing up for vocational training courses at a school in San Francisco. Commissioner of Indian Affairs Dillon Myer was convinced that the relocation program would not be successful unless the government provided Indian relocatees with the training they needed to obtain well-paying jobs.

"PLENTY MORE INDIANS"

Novelist and poet Leslie Marmon Silko has written many works that examine the problems Indians face in contemporary America. In her acclaimed novel, Ceremony, *she tells the story of a young American Indian named Tayo. After surviving the horrors of a Japanese prison camp in World War II, Tayo returns to the Laguna Pueblo reservation in New Mexico. There, like other Indian veterans, he struggles to cope with a sense of alienation from both his own people and from white American society. In the excerpt below, Silko writes of the difficulties encountered by reservation Indians who moved to nearby Gallup, New Mexico, after the war.*

[Tayo] had seen Zunis and Lagunas and Hopis . . . walking alone or in twos and threes along the dusty Gallup streets. He didn't know how they got there in the first place, from the reservation to Gallup, but some must have had jobs for a while when they first came, and cheap rooms on the north side of the tracks, where they stayed until they got laid off or fired. Reservation people were the first ones to get laid off because white people in Gallup already knew they wouldn't ask questions or get angry; they just walked away. They were educated only enough to know they wanted to leave the reservation; when they got to Gallup there weren't many jobs they could get. The men unloaded trucks in the warehouses near the tracks or piled lumber in the lumberyards or pushed wheelbarrows for construction; the women cleaned out motel rooms along Highway 66. The Gallup people knew they didn't have to pay good wages or put up with anything they didn't like, because there were plenty more Indians where these had come from.

friends and relatives who had already moved to cities led some reservation dwellers to learn more about the program. Most of the Indians who applied were young adults. Often they planned to send for their relatives after settling in a city.

Applying for relocation was simple. All an Indian had to do was meet with a relocation worker at an office on or near his or her reservation. The worker evaluated the person's work experience, job preferences, and education background, and then contacted the relocation office in the city to which the applicant wished to move. There were few restrictions on who could apply. An applicant only had to be at least 18 years old and in good health, although applicants with job skills were preferred.

The number of relocation applicants rose dramatically in the early 1950s. By mid-1956, 12,625 reservation Indians had been relocated to urban areas, such as Chicago, Los Angeles, San Francisco,

One of the responsibilities of relocation workers was to find affordable housing for Indians who moved to cities. These Indian men, photographed soon after they arrived in San Jose, were living in a men's boardinghouse.

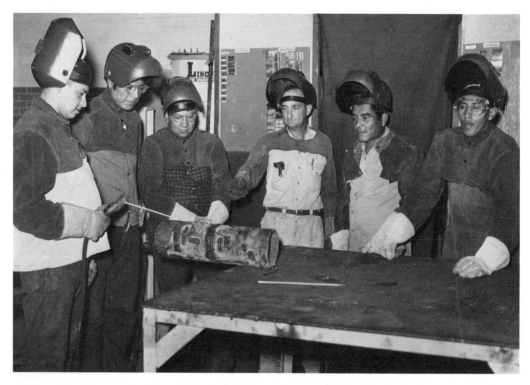

Indians receiving on-the-job training in welding, photographed at Fort Worth, Texas, in the early 1950s.

Denver, San Jose, and St. Louis. When the BIA estimated that another 10,000 applicants would seek assistance before mid-1957, the federal government agreed to triple its relocation funding to almost $3.5 million.

Also in 1956, Congress changed its opinion about job training for relocatees. It passed Public Law 959, which allocated money for several types of vocational education for potential relocatees. One type was on-the-job training, through which an Indian employee could learn a skill by working as an apprentice in a business located near his

or her reservation for two years. Another type trained Indians as carpenters, as plumbers, or as another kind of manual laborer. This training was geared toward adults between the ages of 18 and 35 with families to support. Public Law 959 also initiated a program through which the BIA could negotiate with business firms to build plants near reservations. Such plants could give permanent jobs to reservation residents and teach skills to Indians who wanted eventually to relocate.

The passage of Public Law 959 was the federal government's response to the critics of relocation who claimed that the BIA moved Indians to cities without giving them enough help to find jobs that would allow them to prosper there. The law signaled that the goals of relocation had been readjusted, that job training and placement was now the central aim of the program. The BIA tried to drive this point home by renaming the relocation program the "employment assistance" program. (The bureau may also have wanted to stop critics from linking "relocation" and "removal," the federal policy that had robbed thousands of Indians of their land in the early 19th century. Regardless of the BIA's intentions in changing the program's name, the program was still referred to as relocation by both Indians and BIA workers.)

Indians generally responded well to the government's plan to increase the job training available to them. Many were especially interested in working in the plants the BIA persuaded companies to build near reservations because there Indians could get good jobs without leaving their homes. The BIA had some success finding businesses that wanted to take advantage of the labor pool on Indian lands. But the number of Indians who wanted to work at these plants was far larger than the number of jobs available. Thus, the BIA continued to encourage those who could not find work at reservation industries to relocate.

As the number of relocation applicants grew, so did the amount of money the federal government invested in the program. The funds allocated for relocation became so large that many people in the government began to think that the program's costs were outweighing its benefits. Some congressmen recommended spending money to develop reservation economies instead because it now appeared to be a much cheaper way of providing jobs for Indians.

Between 1952 and 1957, the peak years of the relocation program, about 17,000 Indians received some type of aid from relocation offices. Many more Indians moved to cities without the help of the BIA during this period. The BIA offered optimistic reports on the relocatees' progress. Opponents of the program stated that as many as three out of four relocatees eventually left the city to return to the reservation, but the government denied these statistics. The BIA held that only 3 in 10 relocatees returned to their reservation communities and that half of those who went back did so within 3 months of their move to the city. According to relocation supporters, most Indian relocatees adjusted to a city environment and took advantage of its economic, social, and cultural opportunities to create a richer life than they would have had if they had stayed in an Indian community.

But the most important evaluation of success or failure of the relocation program could not come from BIA employees or government officials. The ultimate judges had to be the relocatees who worked to build a new life in an unfamiliar world. ▲

COME TO DENVER

THE CHANCE OF YOUR LIFETIME!

Good Jobs
Retail Trade
Manufacturing
Government—Federal, State, Local
Wholesale Trade
Construction of Buildings, Etc.

Happy Homes
Beautiful Houses
Many Churches
Exciting Community Life
Over Half of Homes Owned by Residents
Convenient Stores—Shopping Centers

Training
Vocational Training
Auto Mech., Beauty Shop, Drafting,
Nursing, Office Work, Watchmaking
Adult Education
Evening High School, Arts and Crafts
Job Improvement, Home-making

Beautiful Colorado
"Tallest" State, 48 Mt. Peaks Over 14,000 Ft.
350 Days Sunshine, Mild Winters
Zoos, Museums, Mountain Parks, Drives
Picnic Areas, Lakes, Amusement Parks
Big Game Hunting, Trout Fishing, Camping

An example of the promotional literature that BIA relocation workers distributed to reservation Indians encouraging them to move to urban centers.

COPING WITH
CITY LIFE

ome to Denver—The Chance of Your Lifetime!" declared one of the many brochures the BIA produced in the 1950s touting relocation. The brochure also promised Indians "good jobs," "happy homes," and an "exciting community life" in "beautiful Colorado." Other pamphlets made similarly grand claims and often included a photograph of an Indian man in a suit and tie working behind a desk or a smiling Indian woman standing with her children outside a pretty white frame house in the suburbs.

The rosy picture painted by BIA literature bore little resemblance to the harsh realities of city life encountered by the first applicants for relocation. Although each relocatee's experience was different, few found the American dream of a house and a high-paying job as easy to obtain as the BIA had led them to believe it would be.

Some relocatees adjusted to the city with relatively little struggle. Those with job skills or some college education tended to be most successful in making the transition from the reservation to an urban environment because they could generally find work and afford adequate housing. But most relocatees possessed neither of these attributes. They found themselves in a strange world up against obstacles they had had no way of foreseeing. As one relocation authority wrote in 1957, "Relocation is not easy. It calls for real stamina and vigor—adaptability and strength of character."

When a relocatee arrived in the city, he or she was met by a relocation worker. The worker took the Indian shopping for such essentials as groceries and clothing, paid for by the BIA. The bureau also usually covered the Indian's rent and expenses for one

Assimilating Indians into mainstream American society was a major goal of the United States's relocation policy. This BIA photograph of an Indian woman and a white woman with their children was meant to imply that relocatees' adaptation to white society would be easy and beneficial.

month. During this time, the relocation worker tried to help the new arrival find housing, secure a job, and get acclimated to the city. Although the Indian could later call on the worker for counseling or more job placement information, after the first month the relocatees were on their own.

Although relocatees in the early 1950s probably had heard tales of the world outside the reservation from veterans or other Indians who had traveled off the reservation during the war, few had previously encountered a city firsthand. Even modern gadgets city dwellers took for granted were totally new to these Indians. Some relocatees had never seen elevators, telephones, or stoplights.

Even more unsettling than these new objects was the pressure of city life. As in most rural settings, life moved at a fairly slow pace on reservations. The rush of street traffic and the sheer number of people in the city, then, was a shock to many Indians.

In addition to the challenges that most country people face in the city, relocatees had to learn an entirely new concept of time. Mainstream America is made of clock-watchers. Punctuality is praised and tardiness is criticized. In-

dians tend to be less preoccupied by minutes and hours. Instead of living by schedules, they have a flexible approach to time. They may plan to do a certain activity on one day, but if something else comes up they have no problem changing their plans to accommodate it. Frequently plans are interrupted by obligations to friends and kin.

Relocation workers often had newly arrived relocatees buy alarm clocks on their first shopping trip in the city and demonstrated how to use them. But even with such instruction, some relocatees found it difficult to accept the enormous importance non-Indians

THE CHALLENGE OF AN UNKNOWN WORLD

Below, a young Indian woman who arrived in Chicago in 1968 describes her sense of panic in the city—an emotion felt by many of the first relocatees who left their reservation and moved to a large urban area.

Here I am in a big city, right in the middle of Chicago. I don't know anybody. I am so lonesome and I have that urge to go home. I don't know which direction to go—south, north, east or west. I can't just take any direction because I don't know my way around yet.

I see strange faces around me and I keep wondering how I will survive in this strange environment. I keep wondering how I can get over this loneliness, and start adjusting to this environment. I know I have to start somewhere along the line and get involved in social activities and overcome the fear I am holding inside me and replace it with courage, dignity, self-confidence, and the ambition to reach my goal.

Before I can adjust myself to this strange environment and get involved in things, I need friends who will help me overcome this urge to go home so I can accomplish my goal here in this unknown world which I entered.

The BIA often used pictures such as this one of an Indian using modern kitchen appliances to persuade reservation residents to apply for relocation. In the early 1950s, the peak years of relocation, some reservation homes were yet to be equipped with indoor plumbing.

placed on watching the clock and making and keeping appointments. One young Indian man who was attending college courses to improve his chances in the city job market expressed his frustration with following his class schedule in this way: "I nearly went crazy during the first two weeks of college. No matter where I was, I always had to be somewhere else at a certain time. There was no rest."

For some relocatees, the traditional Indian modes of behavior they had been taught as children also made adjusting to city life hard. It is difficult to make accurate generalizations about Indian cultures because they vary greatly; yet, there are some common values among Indian societies that strongly contrast those of white culture. For instance, competitiveness and aggressiveness are esteemed in mainstream American society, whereas Indians value cooperation and generosity. Non-Indian Americans have a long history of stressing the rights and will of the

continued on page 70

THE URBAN INDIAN
IN *HOUSE MADE OF DAWN*

In 1969, Kiowa Indian N. Scott Momaday won the Pulitzer Prize for fiction for his novel House Made of Dawn, *an event that marked the beginning of a renaissance in American Indian literature. Like many of the Indian novelists and poets inspired by his work, Momaday uses his writing to explore the lives of contemporary Indians. One theme that is especially important to Momaday is the struggle of today's Indians to keep their traditions alive in a predominantly non-Indian society.*

House Made of Dawn *tells the story of Abel, an Indian soldier in World War II. After the war, Abel briefly goes back to his reservation before being relocated to Los Angeles. Unable to adjust to city life, he sinks into alcoholism and despair. Only when Abel returns to his homeland and his people does he recover his spirit and sense of purpose.*

Momaday's novel remains one of the most moving accounts of the difficulties encountered by the first generation of Indian relocatees. In the following excerpt, a friend of Abel's in Los Angeles explains simply, but eloquently, the veteran's attempts to cope in an environment he finds unlivable.

It was kind of hard for him, you know, getting used to everything. We had to get down [to the factory] pretty early and put in a day's work. And then at night we would go down to Henry's place and fool around. We would get drunk and have a good time. There were always some girls down there, and on paydays we acted pretty big.

But he was unlucky. Everything went along all right for about two months, I guess. And it would have gone all right after that, too, if they had just let him alone. Maybe . . . you never know about a guy like that; but they wouldn't let him alone. The parole officer, and welfare, and the Relocation people kept coming around, you know, and they were always after him about something. They wanted to know how he was doing, had he been staying out of trouble and all. I guess that got on his nerves after a while, especially the business about drinking and running around. They were

Pultizer Prize–winning novelist N. Scott Momaday, 1988.

always *warning* him, you know? Telling him how he had to stay out of trouble, or else he was going to wind up in prison again. I guess he had to think about that all the time, because they wouldn't let him forget it. Sometimes they talked to me about him, too, and I said he was getting along all right. But he wasn't. And I could see why, but I didn't know how to tell them about it. They wouldn't have understood anyway. You have to get *used* to everything, you know; it's like starting out someplace where you've never been before, and you don't know where you're going or why or when you have to get there, and everybody's looking at you, waiting for you, wondering why you don't hurry up. And they can't help you because you don't know how to talk to them. They have a lot of *words*, and you know they mean something, but you don't know what, and your own words are no good because they're not the same; they're different, and they're the only words you've got. Everything is different, and you don't know how to get used to it. You see the way it is, how everything is going on without you, and you start to worry about it. You wonder how you can get yourself into the swing of it, you know? And you don't know how, but you've got to do it because there's nothing else. And you *want* to do it, because you can see how good it is. It's better than anything you've ever had; it's money and clothes and having plans and going someplace fast. You can *see* what it's like, but you don't know how to get into it; there's too much of it and it's all around you and you can't get hold of it because it's going on too fast. You have to get used to it first, and it's hard. You've got to be left alone. You've got to put a lot of things out of your mind, or you're going to get all mixed up. You've got to take it easy and get drunk once in a while and just forget about who you are. It's hard, and you want to give up. You think about getting out and going home. You want to think that you belong someplace, I guess. You go up there on the hill and you hear the singing and the talk and you think about going home. But the next day you know it's no use; you know that if you went home there would be nothing there, just the empty land and a lot of old people going no place and dying off. And you've got to forget about that, too. Well, they were always coming around and warning him. They wouldn't let him alone, and pretty soon I could see that he was getting all mixed up.

continued from page 66

individual. In contrast, Indians tend to be more community oriented. Being outgoing and adventurous are traits appreciated by non-Indians. Indians, however, are more apt to be reserved and suspicious of strangers.

Some Indian employees quickly learned to act like non-Indians, but others either found it difficult or refused to shed their Indian values. As a result, they were often distrusted by non-Indians, who considered the Indians' quietness and non-aggressiveness as strange, hence threatening, behavior.

Some children of relocatees had similar problems in urban public schools. Uncomfortable with having to compete for grades and sensitive to personal criticism, these Indian students often lost their motivation to do their schoolwork. In some cases, their quiet behavior made them subject to ridicule by their classmates and insensitive teachers. Textbooks that presented Indian stereotypes as truths also contributed to Indian students' unhappiness. Frustrated with their class work and awkward among their peers, many dropped out,

BIA literature frequently showed relocated Indians working at white-collar office jobs. Usually, however, relocatees discovered that the only jobs they could obtain were on factory assembly lines or in service professions, such as waiting tables.

A 1957 BIA photograph of a Chippewa family outside their house in Waukegan, Illinois. In literature distributed by the BIA, its caption read, "This photo shows the kind of house we're talking about in our recent wire. They are available to families now. See your Relocation Officer!"

thereby handicapping their ability to obtain good jobs in the future.

Even if a relocatee adopted non-Indian ways, finding work was a difficult task. Relocation workers referred Indians to companies that agreed to hire recent relocatees, but instead of the white-collar positions suggested by BIA relocation pamphlets, the jobs at these companies were usually in factories. Most of the work was uninteresting, low-paying, and temporary. When many relocatees' BIA funding stopped, they found themselves with barely enough income to survive or with no income at all.

Finding a decent place to live was also an enormous problem for relocatees. Oftentimes, racist landlords re-

fused to rent rooms or apartments to Indians because of old stereotypes that held that all Indians were lazy and dirty. When relocatees found more enlightened landlords, they discovered that they could only afford the rents for apartments in slum areas. Sometimes, to save money, relocatees would share small rented rooms or apartments. Another advantage of living with friends and/or relatives was that newly arrived relocatees had other Indians close by to offer support or advice. But despite this benefit, such crowded conditions were uncomfortable and frustrating, especially to people accustomed to living in a rural area.

In an article in *Atlantic Monthly* magazine, a journalist documented the living conditions of one family of Muscogee Creek Indians who had moved from Oklahoma to Los Angeles. Little Light, her husband Leonard Bear, and their five children were living in "a small shanty" on the outskirts of the city. The dwelling included a "chairless kitchen-dining-living room" where "the walls were unpainted, the floor a patchwork of linoleum." Aside from "a two-burner stove [that] stood on a box . . . the only other piece of furniture in the room [was] a battered table." In the shanty's other room, "three beds were crowded together."

Inadequate housing was not Little Light's only problem with city life. She told her interviewer that her husband spent most nights drinking in a bar where most of the customers were In-

dians. In many cities, Indian bars became the main social centers for area relocatees.

Historically, heavy drinking has been a problem for Indian communities. The reason for this has been debated for many years. Some scholars theorize that biologically Indians are more susceptible to alcoholism. Others believe that, like some people of other impoverished minorities, some Indians are driven to drink by despair and frustration. According to these latter scholars, poverty combined with the disorientation of living in an alien environment make urban Indians prone to look for comfort in alcohol. Yet, it is possible that the alcohol problems of relocatees have been exaggerated. Unlike non-Indian abusers of alcohol, In-

ENCOUNTERING PREJUDICE

*P*rejudice made city life difficult for many relocated Indians. Relocatees were *stereotyped as dirty and lazy and often found that whites were unwilling to hire them or rent them housing. A mother living in the Somerville section of Boston expressed in the late 1960s how a neighbor's prejudice affected her family.*

I won't say that I'm not prejudiced against white people myself sometimes. There are Indians who act worse, though, I know that. But this woman who lived downstairs from us was a real devil. She had a daughter, a big girl about [14 years old]. That girl would pick on [my son] Freddie every time she saw him coming home from school. He'd just be coming home from school and he'd be in his good clothes and all. He does very well at school, don't make no trouble. But this girl would see him coming and she'd tell him, "My mother says that Indians is no good" . . . She had no business doing that. She went on and on about "dirty Indians."

A Navajo woman and her six children, photographed in their Los Angeles home in the late 1950s. Claiming that the "entire family have progressed steadily and are well adjusted to the Los Angeles area," the BIA used the image to advertise the relocation program.

dians rarely drink alone because they view drinking primarily as a social activity. Because Indian drinking is public drinking, their alcohol consumption might be more obvious than that of other Americans but not any greater. In any case, the existence of Indian bars unfortunately became an excuse for racists to promote another old stereotype, that of the "drunken Indian." As a result, the many relocatees who rarely or never consumed alcohol were sometimes unfairly assumed to be heavy drinkers by prospective employers and landlords.

Little Light also complained of another problem common to urban Indians—obtaining quality health care. One of her children was sick but she did not have enough money to take the child to a doctor. Many other relocatees shared her predicament, a problem

THE HIGH COST OF CITY LIFE

The primary reason many Indians choose to relocate to an urban area is to improve their standard of living. To the surprise of many of the relocatees of the 1950s and 1960s, however, low-paying jobs and high-priced goods made it impossible for them to prosper in the city. One Navajo who moved to Denver in 1966 expressed his frustration with the high cost of city life in this way:

When I came to Denver I didn't think I'd have much trouble after a while. I had a lot of money, but that was before I bought that car. It was a '59 Ford. After we bought that car it seems like the money just go by. . . .

So I think that the most important thing that a man has is to have money. I have found in Denver that things are too high. Everything. Groceries, clothing, gas, and everything else is too high.

magnified by the high incidence of several serious illnesses, such as diabetes and glaucoma, among Indian peoples. Reservation Indians generally received free health care financed by the federal government. But once Indians moved to a city, either on their own or through the relocation program, they were told they were no longer eligible for this benefit.

Doctor bills were but one of the many expenses of city life that surprised urban Indians. Many of the first relocatees were shocked by the high cost of rent, food, clothing, and other essentials. Even with the low pay of most of the jobs available to them, Indians in the city usually could make more money than they had on the reservation. But the cost of urban living was so high that often they were some-

times poorer after relocation. Instead of finding a better life in the city, they discovered that they had merely traded reservation poverty for urban poverty.

For many Indians, relocation proved to be a failure. No better off financially than before, they gave up on the city and moved back to their reservations. But some relocatees who succeeded in raising their standard of living also made the decision to return. Their reasons for leaving also varied. The noise and filth of the city made some people move home. Others missed their families. Still others decided that they did not want to live among non-Indians and adopt their ways. Some cited all these reasons and more.

But many relocatees chose to remain in the city despite all the problems they

A Cherokee man in this BIA photograph is shown shopping for a jacket. Although availability of modern goods attracted some early relocatees to cities, their low wages often prohibited them from purchasing anything other than essentials.

encountered. Some took to the city, enjoying the air of excitement that confirmed urban dwellers tend to crave. Some cited that an urban setting offered better schools for their children and greater employment opportunities for themselves. Others merely did not want to live on a reservation and felt that urban life was the best alternative.

In its early years, the relocation program helped some Indians and hurt others. But whether they elected to stay in the city or to return home, the examples of the early relocatees made the transition from reservation to urban life easier for all of those Indians who followed them. The first relocatees had no choice but to be trailblazers. Now Indians who move to the city can trace the paths they forged. ▲

An Indian boy dancing during the three-day Denver March Pow Wow in 1986.

URBAN INDIANS
TODAY

In the early 1960s, the administration of President John F. Kennedy announced its intention to provide aid to Americans mired in poverty. With this goal in mind, Kennedy appointed Philleo Nash the commissioner of Indian affairs in 1961. Trained as an anthropologist and with many years of government service behind him, Nash was determined to raise the standard of living of Indians across the nation.

One of Nash's goals was to end the termination of federal responsibilities to tribes. Between 1954 and 1962, 61 Indian groups had been terminated. The experiences of the members of these groups proved termination to be one of the most misguided policies in the history of the government's dealings with Indian people. Instead of becoming self-sufficient when "freed" from government interference in their affairs,

most terminated tribes suffered horribly from increased poverty and unemployment because of their sudden loss of federally funded services. In addition to the misery it caused thousands of Indians, the termination policy failed in its goal to save the government money. In the end, the cost of welfare payments made to impoverished terminated Indians far exceeded the price of the services provided to them before termination.

Becoming frustrated with their treatment from the federal government, American Indians from urban and reservation areas began to mount a national protest. Professors Sol Tax, Nancy Lurie, and others helped to organize a week-long meeting held near the University of Chicago and attended by more than 450 Indians representing 90 tribes. After discussing their common problems, the conference participants announced their own Indian policy calling for more control over their life.

To the relief of Indians across the United States, the termination policy was abandoned in the 1960s. The relocation program, however, grew substantially during the same period. Between 1950 and 1959, the government allocated $20 million for relocation. Between 1960 and 1969, relocation expenditures grew to $121 million. In 1969 alone, the amount of money devoted to relocation was greater than the total expenditures for the program throughout the entire 1950s.

Like termination, relocation had its critics. Both Indians and non-Indians claimed that government workers had coerced reservation dwellers into moving to cities with false promises and then had done little to help the relocatees cope with their new environment. The increased amount of funds spent on each relocatee in the 1960s was intended to counter some of these attacks. The BIA now paid for moving expenses of relocatees, living expenses until they had a steady job and a regular paycheck, and an increased range of counseling services. In 1967, the government also began to offer relocatees grants to help them make a down payment on a house. These new services helped a large number of relocatees adjust to the city. However, the many Indians who moved to urban areas without applying to the relocation program

were still denied any assistance from the BIA.

In addition to a larger budget for the relocation program, the experiences of the earlier relocatees were an enormous help to Indians who moved from reservations to cities after 1960. Many Indians who relocated to urban areas in the late 1940s and 1950s were ill prepared for their new environment. Those who followed them, however, generally knew what to expect, largely because of what they had heard from or about the first relocatees. Also, by the 1960s reservation communities were much less isolated from the outside world than they had been in the late 1940s and early 1950s. Television played a large role in this change. Too expensive to be purchased by most Americans just after the war, televisions were commonplace in even poor reservation communities 15 years later. Through television and other mass media, later Indian relocatees learned a lot about cities long before they had ever set foot in one.

When these relocatees arrived in the city, they were likely to move into neighborhoods with large concentrations of Indians. These Indian enclaves had grown up in poor sections of cities because only these areas were affordable to poorly paid Indian laborers. In many of these neighborhoods, the BIA established Indian centers, which often replaced bars as the focus of social activity for Indian residents. Although these neighborhoods usually offered

EVALUATING RELOCATION

The federal government's relocation program drew varied reactions from both Indians and non-Indians. Below are two views recorded by anthropologist Merwyn S. Garbarino in the late 1960s. The first came from a 24-year-old Indian woman; the second, from a 25-year-old Indian man.

I came under the relocation program. I applied through the agency back on the reservation, and I came to Chicago to go to school. I went to a business school in a suburb, and I liked it out there. It was really beautiful, lived at the Y. We don't any more.

I took secretarial training, and some of the teachers were good and some weren't. I used to think . . . I still think that sometimes they just passed us with good grades because they knew the BIA would go on paying. So maybe we really didn't get a very good education always. But I must have learned all right because I applied for a job as a secretary, and I got it OK, and I am still doing it. I think the relocation program is a good thing, but the BIA just never seems to do anything right. They really don't seem to take an interest in the students, and they ran us through like cattle, but the idea is still good. And some of the advisors are real nice and helpful. Well, anyhow, I have a job now that pays enough and I can save some money. It is my hope to go to college someday.

I don't like living in Chicago. I'm here on the relocation training program, and I'm glad to learn a trade, but I sure don't like the city. The BIA doesn't give us enough money to live in Chicago. It's awfully expensive here. But it's not just that. People are different here—even the Indians. They don't talk to you. . . . I got lost on the "el" [elevated train] and no one would help me. City people are in such a hurry. As soon as I finish school, I'm going away— maybe back to the reservation, but to a small town anyhow. I'd rather be in a small town and not have such a good job [than] stay in the city.

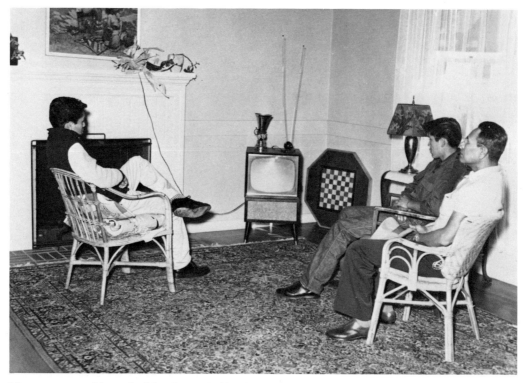

Three men watching television in an Oakland, California, boardinghouse in the late 1950s. Television provided important information about cities to the second generation of Indian relocatees.

poor living conditions, they eased the relocatees' transition to city life. Instead of being thrown into non-Indian society, relocatees in the 1960s could choose to move into areas where most of their neighbors were Indians.

In these enclaves, people retained many of their traditional ways. This fact proved untrue one of the assumptions of BIA officials who supported relocation—that all Indians who moved to cities wanted to assimilate into the mainstream culture. Actually most relocatees were motivated to leave their homes

purely for economic reasons. Many wanted to take advantage of the job opportunities of cities, but, if given a choice, did not want to abandon their traditional culture completely. In some ways, Indian neighborhoods offered later relocatees this alternative.

Some urban Indians developed another strategy that allowed them to work in the city but also retain a tribal way of life. These people took temporary, seasonal jobs in fields such as construction. When they were working, they lived in the city. During the time of year that work was unavailable, they moved back to their reservation. This way of living resembled that of Indian traders long ago, who often had to leave their communities to travel to non-Indian populated settlements to deal with non-Indian traders. The most well known group of Indians who choose to divide their time between the city and the reservation are Mohawk steelworkers. They are responsible for constructing the steel framework of many tall buildings in American cities.

With increased federal spending on reservations, Indians in a few areas discovered that they did not need to leave their homes to become urbanized. The economic development created small urban centers on or near reservations, such as Tuba City in Arizona. By the mid-1960s, many Hopi Indians from the nearby village of Moenkopi commuted to Tuba City to work or to engage in social activities such as watching movies or attending dances. Comfortable with city ways through their experiences in Tuba City, many regularly took the two-hour trip by car to shop in Flagstaff, a fairly large city populated primarily by non-Indians. By living in Moenkopi, working in Tuba City, and visiting Flagstaff, these Hopi reaped the benefits both of their traditional culture and of urban life.

For those Indians who did want to assimilate, the example of Indians who had already settled in non-Indian urban neighborhoods made that path easier than ever. Working as teachers, as lawyers, or in other professions, some In-

Two Mohawk Indians putting an iron girder in place in a Manhattan skyscraper. Since the mid-1950s, hundreds of Mohawk have found jobs in construction in the New York City area.

dians established themselves in esteemed fields dominated by whites and made high enough salaries to afford housing in relatively affluent areas. These successful Indians inspired others who wanted to achieve a high standard of living and to adopt a similar way of life. Even Indians who did not want to live like these professionals shared their pride in their accomplishments.

Indians developed a variety of ways of living in the city. But even with these different life-styles, as time passed, ur-

WHO IS AN INDIAN?

In the eyes of the federal government, an Indian is a person with one-fourth Indian ancestry. But for many urban Indians, especially those born in the city, defining exactly what it means to be Indian is far more complex. In the following quotes, two Native American city dwellers explain their personal definitions of Indianness.

Being an Indian to me is being myself. What person knows what has made him? I guess people of French or any other European ancestry feel the same way. Or Orientals. I don't think it is really different. It means that you belong to something, a group or some tradition. There are so many different kinds of traditions and I don't know that one is better than another. Seems to me that the important thing is you know yourself.

I think it is something you can choose, whether to be an Indian or not. I mean you can choose if you have grown up in the city. It's probably not the same thing if you are reservation-bred because there would be stronger ties to Indian identity, whatever that is. But anyhow, in my case, you can say that I am just a Chicagoan.

ban Indians had more in common with each other than with their reservation kin. City dwellers tended to be less traditional, in part because it was difficult to retain ancient Indian ways in an urban setting. Another factor, though, was that affiliation with a tribe was much less important in the city. Usually people of many different tribes lived together in Indian neighborhoods. Their close contact broke down most of the traditional barriers between Indian groups. For instance, the Navajo and the Hopi of the Southwest had long regarded each other as enemies because of land disputes between them. In the city, these old arguments seemed less

relevant. The shared experience of Navajo and Hopi urban dwellers as part of the Indian minority in a primarily non-Indian city population drew these people closer together than the disputes of their tribes tore them apart. In contrast, membership in a particular tribe remained central to most reservation Indians' sense of identity. The majority of reservations housed only one tribe. Most reservation Indians had relatively little contact with people of other tribes and, when they did, they regarded Indians with other tribal affiliations as being very different from themselves.

Political developments during the 1960s further separated urban Indians and reservation Indians. During the presidencies of John F. Kennedy and Lyndon B. Johnson, government funding for social services for Indians rose substantially. The BIA had long been criticized for being insensitive to Indians' needs. To counter further complaints, the United States allowed tribal governments to have much more say than ever before on how this money was to be spent. Urban Indians who lived far away from their reservations had relatively little influence over tribal officials. City dwellers consequently grew bitter, believing that reservation tribespeople were drawing many more benefits from government aid to Indians than they were.

Reservation Indians, in turn, had reason to resent their relatives in cities.

A protest against the policies of the federal government was held in Denver, Colorado, in 1970.

Members of the American Indian Movement during the militant group's 1973 takeover of the town of Wounded Knee, South Dakota.

Traditionalists often felt that urban Indians had turned their back on their heritage by living among non-Indians. They also were angry that cities lured away many of the most ambitious and educated Indian youths. This brain drain frustrated reservation Indians efforts to develop their tribal economies.

Isolated from tribal governments and excluded from city politics, angry young urban Indians began to form organizations in the late 1960s to combat the injustices they saw in American society. These organizations drew strength and inspiration from the civil rights movement, which sought fair treatment for all minorities. Most of the groups were openly hostile toward the BIA, a stance that distinguished them from tribal governments. Although tribal governments were often critical of the BIA, they generally had to work with the bureau in order to obtain funding.

Among the political groups founded by urban Indians during this period were the American Indian Movement (AIM), formed in 1968 in Minneapolis,

Minnesota, and the United Native Americans, Inc., established in 1969 in San Francisco, California. These and other Indian organizations were involved in public protests against the policies of the federal government.

Probably the most publicized Indian protest of the period took place in the town of Wounded Knee on the Pine Ridge Sioux Reservation in South Dakota. (Wounded Knee was the location of a 1890 massacre of hundreds of Sioux men, women, and children at the hands of U.S. soldiers.) On February 27, 1973, 200 members of AIM took over the town and used the press coverage of the seizure to voice their complaints against tribal leaders. The occupation of Wounded Knee continued for 71 days until the AIM members were ousted by the FBI and federal marshals.

The actions of urban Indian militants—dubbed the Red Power movement by the media—had some negative effects. In the minds of many non-Indians, the stereotype of the Indian warrior on horseback familiar from movie westerns was replaced by the stereotype of the hostile Indian militant. Many Indians did not support AIM and other urban Indian political organizations and, therefore, resented that the organizations had come to represent all Indian people to most other Americans. The organizations' criticism of tribal governments also increased the growing gulf between urban and reservation Indians.

The so-called Red Power movement, however, did awaken pride in

At the height of the Red Power movement, Indian demonstrators took control of the BIA offices in Washington, D.C.

many Native Americans. With a renewed interest in their heritage and history, they began to revive uniquely Indian art, literature, music, and dance. For the many urban Indians who had no strong tribal affiliation, this revitalization movement led them to celebrate their "Indianness" rather than an association with one particular Indian group. Through Pan-Indianism, urban Indians banded together to combat the prejudices that had lowered their self-esteem in the past.

THE BIRTH OF AIM

Clyde Bellacourt, a young Ojibwa man, had a troubled life. As a boy in reform school, he learned to steal cars. By his late teens, he had mastered breaking into houses. Now he was serving time in Minnesota's Stillwater State Prison for burglary. Depressed and defeated, Bellacourt was convinced that he was "an ignorant, dirty savage." Sitting alone in his cell, he "just gave up" on his future.

Bellacourt's fortune changed when Eddie Benton, a Stillwater trustee, began to visit him. An Ojibwa himself, Benton saw something familiar in Bellacourt's depression. Like other Indian youths Benton knew, the inmate seemed crushed by living in non-Indian society. "The system beats Indian people down," Benton concluded. "It robs them of their self-respect."

During his visits, Benton told Bellacourt about the Ojibwa people, about their noble history and their great spirituality. From listening to Benton, the young man learned to be proud rather than ashamed of his heritage. "For the first time in my life, I realized that I wasn't a savage. I wasn't filthy and I wasn't ignorant. I was smart and capable." With Benton, Bellacourt founded an organization at Stillwater to help other Indian inmates learn to draw strength from their Indian identity.

After leaving prison in 1964, Bellacourt moved to Franklin Avenue in Minneapolis, a neighborhood with a large concentration of Indians. Firsthand, he saw a wealth of social problems afflicting the area. Although there were already nearly 30 Indian organizations in the vicinity, Bellacourt believed conditions were getting worse rather than better. He and another ex-con, Dennis Banks, joined together to form the American Indian Movement (AIM), a group of Minneapolis Indians committed to improving their community.

The first issue addressed by AIM members was police brutality. There had been several incidents in the Franklin Avenue area in which Indians had been beaten by white policemen. AIM formed a patrol that, with cameras in hand, traveled to the scene of the arrest of any Indian to photograph the behavior of the police. Afraid of having the beatings they inflicted documented, most of the guilty policemen ceased brutalizing Indian victims.

In its early years, AIM had many other successes. Among them was creating an alcohol rehabilitation program, founding a school for Indian students, and establishing a health board that provided emergency housing for the poor. And, like the organization Bellacourt founded at Stillwater, AIM helped to restore its members' pride in being Indian. In the words of Dennis Banks, "I think that all of the injustices that have been occurring to Indian people led me to believe that Indian people would have to take a stand or perish. . . . In Minneapolis, we organized the American Indian Movement to take such a stand."

AIM grew quickly, as chapters were established in many cities. At the same time, the scope of its ambitions increased. Rather than concerning themselves with just the problems of urban Indians in Minneapolis, AIM members sought to reform the treatment of all American Indians. Through several highly publicized protests, including the 1973 occupation of Wounded Knee, AIM became the most well known militant Indian group in the country.

In 1988, AIM celebrated its 20th anniversary. Since its birth, the organization has inspired controversy. Many Indians have applauded its efforts to create radical change. But many others have complained that AIM's demands and claims only represent the opinions of a minority of Indian people. Although the merits of AIM's tactics and desires are still debated, it has clearly succeeded in one goal—to give a voice to the frustration and anger felt by all Indians.

The celebration of the 20th anniversary of the founding of AIM.

A medicine man (right) treating Indian leader Richard Oakes in a San Francisco hospital in 1970. Although many urban Indians still use traditional medicines and cures, they also demand that the government address their dire need for Western quality health care.

The Indian activism of the late 1960s and early 1970s, however, was also very effective in drawing attention to many of the problems of Indians that had previously been ignored. It helped to usher in a new federal policy—self-determination—which held that Indian people should be allowed to decide for themselves how best to live. The policy di-rectly opposed the forced assimilation of the termination era and gave Indians even more power to oversee how the money allocated to them was spent.

In some ways, self-determination has allowed Indians to build a better future for themselves. For instance, since the beginning of the 1970s, great progress has been made in Indian health care. With the passage of the Indian Health Care Improvement Act in 1976, Congress budgeted $355 million to combat the health crises that had long plagued Indian communities. This legislation stipulated that some of this money was to be devoted to "a program of contracts with Indian organizations in urban areas for the purpose of making health services more accessible to Indians." The result of this measure has been the establishment of Indian health centers in Milwaukee, Detroit, Seattle, Minneapolis, Phoenix, and Los Angeles. Special clinics for Indians also exist in most other major American urban areas.

Government efforts to improve Indian education have been less successful. Students in reservation schools

A worker at the Native American Counseling Center in New York offering advice to an Indian man. Indian centers in cities throughout the United States provide information and aid to urban Indians in need of improved housing, education, jobs, and health care.

90

MAJOR URBAN INDIAN POPULATION CENTERS

Duluth

St. Paul

Minneapolis

Sioux Falls

Yankton

Sioux City

Omaha

Milwaukee

Madison

Grand
Rapids

Lansing

Detroit

Chicago

Cleveland

Topeka

Kansas City

Wichita

Tulsa

Muskogee

Oklahoma
City

Dallas

Baton Rouge

Houston

New Orleans

Bangor

Boston

Rochester

Buffalo

Albany

Hartford

New York
City

Pittsburgh

Harrisburg

Philadelphia

Baltimore

Washington

Charlotte

Asheville

Three teenage graduates of the Heart of the Earth Survival School in Minneapolis, Minnesota.

have benefited from increased Indian input in developing classroom curricula. Indian children attending city schools, however, still must contend with the prejudices of teachers and with school systems that generally do not take their special needs into consideration. High dropout rates among urban Indian youths continue to be a problem.

Job training programs have also failed to provide adult Indians with the education they need. Since the late 1950s, a high percentage of Indians enrolled in vocational courses have not completed them. Some of the dropouts complain that they were coerced into taking courses offering training in fields in which there are few available jobs or in occupations in which the students have no interest. Others responded poorly to pressure placed on them by unsympathetic instructors. These problems with Indian vocational training have helped to make the unemployment rate of urban Indians more than double that of the American population as a whole. Although an increasing number of urban Indians are establishing themselves in high-salaried professions, most of those who do have jobs receive relatively low pay. As a result, the average Indian family income according to the 1980 census was only $13,869. In comparison, the income of the average white family was found to be $20,927.

In the 1980s, the Reagan administration cut federal funding to Indian groups by almost 40 percent. This cut in spending has hurt all Indians, but urban Indians have been affected the most. As in the past, some U.S. officials continue to argue that Indians living in cities are in need of and entitled to the same type of special services the federal government provides for many reservation Indians. As urban Indians have lost access to government-funded educational assistance and health care, they have increasingly asked their

HOPE FOR THE FUTURE

Dr. Henrietta Whiteman, a Cheyenne educator on the faculty of the University of Montana, has lived both on reservations and in cities. In the following excerpt from her 1975 speech, "Spiritual Roots of Indian Success," she expresses her hope for a better future for all Indian peoples.

We, as Native Americans, have our own unique philosophical concepts. Our cultural heritage was and is rich because of our tribal diversities. This country was, indeed, the "promised land"—it still is. I say *it is*, for now there is the glimmer of growing respect for cultural differences, as well as for tribal or individual differences. Today, I am witnessing a change in attitude where it is no longer inferior to be different; but to be different is good. The myth of the "melting pot" has proven to be a myth. Many people have recognized the disorientation of society in general, and they are seeking a new direction. This world will become a better place in which to live when society recognizes what we, as Native Americans, have always known.

An Indian teacher instructs a multiracial class in Minneapolis about the dangers of stereotyping people of other ethnic backgrounds. Today, urban Indians continue to fight prejudice while making important contributions to the cities they now call home.

tribes to make tribal services open to them. Because of the past differences between reservation and urban Indians, such requests are not always honored. It remains to be seen whether, in the future, Indians living in different areas and with different ways of life will be able to pull together to work for the betterment of all Indian peoples.

One encouraging sign is the interaction of reservation and urban Indians at powwows. These large gatherings attract Indians from many tribes as well as non-Indian tourists with exhibitions of Indian crafts and displays of Indian singing and dancing. Some powwows are held on reservation land, but they are also becoming popular in cities. Several large powwows are held annually in Chicago, Albuquerque, Denver, and Oklahoma City. These events provide urban Indians who grew up in the city with a way of learning about their heritage and of meeting Indians of other backgrounds.

Whether by finding strength in their roots or by adopting others' city ways as their own, urban Indians for decades have created innovative strategies for thriving as city dwellers. Drawing on their experiences, their children and grandchildren in the next century will develop new, possibly even better, solutions to building a quality life in an environment often indifferent to their needs. They, however, will have to face problems their elders did not, as social and economic conditions in America's cities worsen. But, like their ancestors, these new urban Indians will no doubt seek out and find unique paths toward prosperity in the ever-changing city. ▲

BIBLIOGRAPHY

Fixico, Donald L. *Termination and Relocation: Federal Indian Policy, 1945–1960*. Albuquerque: University of New Mexico Press, 1986.

Hertzberg, Hazel. *The Search for an American Indian Identity, Modern Pan-Indian Movements*. Syracuse: University of Syracuse Press, 1971.

Levine, Stuart, and Nancy O. Lurie, eds. *American Indians Today*. Baltimore: Penguin Books, 1968.

Neils, Elaine. *Reservation to City: Indian Migration and Federal Relocation*. Chicago: University of Chicago, 1971.

Sorkin, Alan. *The Urban American Indian*. Lexington: Lexington Books, 1978.

Steiner, Stan. *The New Indians*. New York: Delta Books, 1968.

Thorton, Russell. *The Urbanization of American Indians: A Critical Bibliography*. Bloomington: Indiana University Press, 1982.

Waddell, Jack, and O. Michael Watson, eds. *The American Indian in Urban Society*. Boston: Little, Brown, 1971.

GLOSSARY

agent A person appointed by the Bureau of Indian Affairs to supervise U.S. government programs on a reservation and/or in a specific region. After 1908 the title *superintendent* replaced *agent*.

agriculture Intensive cultivation of tracts of land, sometimes using draft animals and heavy plowing equipment. Agriculture requires a largely nonnomadic life.

allotment U.S. policy applied nationwide through the General Allotment Act passed in 1887, aimed at breaking up tribally owned reservations by assigning individual farms and ranches to Indians. Allotment was intended as much to discourage traditional communal activities as to encourage private farming and assimilate Indians into mainstream American life.

American Indian Movement (AIM) A group formed in 1968 by urban Indian political activists in Minneapolis, Minnesota, whose goals were to gain fulfillment of U.S. treaty obligations to American Indians and to increase federal programs to support impoverished Indian families. AIM members staged a series of building takeovers, including one at Alcatraz prison, to focus media attention of the plight of American Indians.

anthropology The study of the physical, social, and historical characteristics of human beings.

assimilation The complete absorption of one group into another group's cultural tradition.

Bureau of Indian Affairs (BIA) A U.S. government agency now within the Department of the Interior. Originally intended to manage trade and other relations with Indians, the BIA today seeks to develop and implement programs that encourage Indians to manage their own affairs and to improve their educational opportunities and general social and economic well-being.

culture The learned behavior of humans; nonbiological, socially taught activities; the way of life of a group of people.

Department of the Interior U.S. government office created in 1849 to oversee the internal affairs of the United States, including government land sales, land-related legal disputes, and American Indian issues.

General Allotment Act An act passed by Congress in 1887 that provided for the division of Indian reservations into individually owned tracts of land.

House Concurrent Resolution 108 A 1953 law that aimed to terminate the financial support and services that the federal government had pledged to give Indians in past treaties.

Indian Claims Commission (ICC) A U.S. government body created by an act of Congress in 1946 to hear and rule on claims brought by Indians against the United States. These claims stem from unfulfilled treaty terms, such as nonpayment for lands sold by the Indians.

Indian Removal Act An 1830 federal law that authorized the resettlement of eastern Indian tribes to new lands west of the Mississippi River.

Indian Reorganization Act (IRA) A 1934 federal law that ended the policy of allotting plots of land to individuals and encouraged the development of reservation communities. The act also provided for the creation of autonomous tribal governments.

Indian Territory An area in the south-central United States to which the U.S. government wanted to resettle Indians from other regions, especially the eastern states. In 1907, this area and Oklahoma Territory became the state of Oklahoma.

Meriam Report A 1928 federal government study that disclosed the horrendous state of health care, education, and the economy in Indian communities and recommended several reforms in federal Indian policy.

missionaries Advocates of a particular religion who travel to convert nonbelievers to their faith.

Pan-Indian movement A renewed interest in Indian identity that spread throughout North America in the early decades of the 20th century.

powwow An Indian social gathering that includes feasting, dancing, rituals, and arts and crafts displays, to which other Indian groups as well as non-Indians are now often invited.

Red Power movement A series of organized public demonstrations in the late 1960s and early 1970s by militant urban Indians to protest against the policies of the federal government.

relocation A U.S. policy of the late 20th century that encouraged Indians to leave reservations and migrate to the cities in order to enter mainstream society.

removal policy A federal policy, initiated in 1830, that called for the sale of all Indian land in the eastern and southern United States and the migration of Indians from these areas to lands west of the Mississippi River.

reservation, reserve A tract of land retained by Indians for their own occupation and use. *Reservation* is used to describe such lands in the United States; *reserve*, in Canada.

self-determination The federal government's current Indian policy, which gives tribes freedom to choose whether to remain on reservations, to form tribal governments, and to assume responsibility for services traditionally provided by the BIA.

stereotype A standardized mental picture held in common by some people, representing an oversimplified opinion, affective attitude, or uncritical judgment.

termination Federal policy to remove Indian tribes from government supervision and Indian lands from government control. Termination was in effect from the late 1940s through the early 1960s.

treaty A contract negotiated between representatives of the U.S. government or another national government and one or more Indian tribes. Treaties dealt with the cessation of military action, the surrender of political independence, the establishment of boundaries, terms of land sales, and related matters.

tribalism The maintenance of traditional Indian ways of life.

tribe A society consisting of several or many separate communities united by kinship, culture, language, and other social institutions including clans, religious organizations, and warrior societies.

INDEX

DEDICATION

To my parents, John L. and Virginia L. Fixico

ACKNOWLEDGMENT

Excerpt from *House Made of Dawn* by N. Scott Momaday. Copyright © 1968 by N. Scott Momaday. Reprinted by permission of HarperCollins Publishers.

PICTURE CREDITS

DONALD L. FIXICO is professor of history at Western Michigan University. After receiving his Ph.D. in history in 1980, he received two postdoctoral fellowships—one at the Newberry Library in Chicago and the other at the American Indian Studies Center of the University of California at Los Angeles. He has taught as a visiting professor at several universities and his research focuses on American Indians in the 20th century. Dr. Fixico is the author of many articles and two books, *Termination and Relocation: Federal Indian Policy, 1945–1960* and *An Anthology of Western Great Lakes Indian History.*

FRANK W. PORTER III, general editor of INDIANS OF NORTH AMERICA, is director of the Chelsea House Foundation for American Indian Studies. He holds a B.A., M.A., and Ph.D. from the University of Maryland. He has done extensive research concerning the Indians of Maryland and Delaware and is the author of numerous articles on their history, archaeology, geography, and ethnography. He was formerly director of the Maryland Commission on Indian Affairs and American Indian Research and Resource Institute, Gettysburg, Pennsylvania, and he has received grants from the Delaware Humanities Forum, the Maryland Committee for the Humanities, the Ford Foundation, and the National Endowment for the Humanities, among others. Dr. Porter is the author of *The Bureau of Indian Affairs* in the Chelsea House KNOW YOUR GOVERNMENT series.